AF693382

Bridging AI and Law

A Practical Guide for Lawyers and Technologists

TOLULOPE AWOYOMI

AI Curators Press

Bridging AI and Law: A Practical Guide for Lawyers and Technologists

Second Edition 2026

Copyright © 2026 by Tolulope Awoyomi

All rights reserved. No part of this publication may be translated, reprinted, reproduced, stored in a retrieval system, or transmitted in any form or by any means, including electronic, mechanical, photocopying, recording, or otherwise, without prior written permission from the publisher. This includes reuse of illustrations, broadcasting, electronic adaptation, computer software, or any similar or dissimilar methodology now known or developed in the future.

ISBN: 979-8-9996774-5-7

The mention of trade names, trademarks, service marks, or similar terms in this publication, even when not specifically identified, should not be interpreted as indicating whether such terms are protected by proprietary rights.

Every effort has been made to ensure the accuracy of the information contained in this book at the time of publication. However, neither the author, the editors, nor the publisher assumes any legal responsibility for errors or omissions. The publisher makes no warranty, express or implied, regarding the content.

Published by AI Curators Press

Washington, DC, USA

info@aicuratorspress.com

aicuratorspress.com

CONTENTS

To my parents: Engr. Johnson Awoyomi and Adenike Awoyomi
To my siblings: Abiola Awoyomi and Adeola Awoyomi
Thank you for always being there.

INTRODUCTION

A piece of evidence appears real. The video is clear. The voice is convincing. The details align. It looks authentic, sounds authentic, and fits seamlessly into a narrative that makes sense. But it never happened.

This is the reality artificial intelligence introduces into modern legal systems. Evidence can now be generated, altered, or simulated with a level of precision that challenges one of the most fundamental assumptions of law: that what we see can be trusted. For decades, legal systems have operated on relatively stable foundations. Documents could be authenticated, images could be examined, and testimony could be challenged. While deception has always existed, it operated within limits. Artificial intelligence removes many of those limits.

The challenge is no longer determining whether something is false. It is whether trust itself can still be established in a world where reality can be manufactured. At the same time, artificial intelligence is not operating outside the law. It is embedded within it. AI systems are already shaping decisions about hiring, lending, healthcare, policing, and legal outcomes.[1] These systems are not abstract technologies. They are decision-making infrastructures that affect rights, opportunities, and accountability in real and measurable ways. Yet there is a structural problem at the center of this transformation.

Artificial intelligence is advancing within a disconnect between two professions that increasingly shape how decisions are made in society. Technologists build systems that

---

1. OECD, *Artificial Intelligence in Society* (2019); World Economic Forum, *Global Risk Report: AI and Decision Systems* (2023).

learn, predict, and act. Lawyers interpret rules, assign responsibility, and protect rights. Both operate with rigor, yet they do not operate in the same way, and more importantly, they do not move at the same speed.

This divergence has created a gap that is no longer theoretical. It is operational. It is already influencing who gets hired, who gets approved for credit, whose data is used, and who is held accountable when systems fail. The challenge is not simply that artificial intelligence introduces new risks. The deeper issue is that those risks are emerging in a space where technical capability and legal oversight are not yet aligned.

> **Key Idea:**
> The most significant risks in artificial intelligence do not arise from what the technology can do, but from the gap between those who build systems and those who regulate them.

Technologists are trained to optimize. Their work is driven by performance, efficiency, and scale. When a system processes data efficiently and produces accurate outputs, it is considered successful. Lawyers, by contrast, are trained to interrogate systems. Their focus is not only on outcomes, but on how those outcomes are reached, whether the process is fair, and whether it can be justified within existing legal frameworks.

Where technologists ask whether something works, lawyers ask whether it is acceptable. These perspectives are not in conflict. They are complementary. Yet in practice, they are often separated.

This separation is rooted in how each discipline is trained to think. Engineering culture rewards speed, iteration, and improvement. Legal culture rewards caution, reasoning, and justification. One is oriented towards building an advanced future. The other is grounded in interpreting the past while also creating a regulated and predictable future. Artificial intelligence forces these two orientations into direct contact, and the result is tension. When systems are built without legal foresight, risks become embedded in the architecture itself. When legal systems attempt to respond after deployment, they struggle to catch up with systems already operating at scale.

At its core, this is a problem of timing. Technology moves forward through deployment. Law moves forward through interpretation. By the time legal systems fully understand a technology, it is often already widely adopted.

Artificial intelligence does not simply change how decisions are made. It changes the scale at which decisions operate. A human error is typically limited in scope, affecting a single individual or a small number of outcomes. An algorithmic error, by contrast, can be replicated across thousands or even millions of decisions within a short period of time. A recruiter may overlook a candidate. An algorithm may exclude an entire category of candidates. A loan officer may exercise bias in a single decision. A lending model may encode that bias across thousands of approvals. This is the defining shift.

Key Insight:

AI does not just automate decisions. It automates patterns, and once those patterns are embedded, they become systems.

Artificial intelligence does not introduce entirely new forms of bias or error. It amplifies existing ones and distributes them at a scale that was previously impossible. What begins as a pattern becomes a system, and once embedded in a system, it becomes difficult to detect and even harder to reverse.

At the same time, many artificial intelligence systems operate in ways that are difficult to fully explain. Machine learning models, particularly those built on complex architectures, do not always provide clear reasoning for their outputs. Even their creators may not be able to trace precisely how a particular decision was reached. This creates a direct conflict with the expectations of the law.

Legal systems depend on explanation. They depend on the ability to reconstruct decisions, assign reasoning, and evaluate whether that reasoning meets established standards. Artificial intelligence systems, by contrast, often produce results without narratives. They offer conclusions without explanations. This is not simply a technical limitation. It is a structural mismatch.

Critical Observation:

The law asks "why." AI often answers with "because the data suggests so" (statistical correlation).

Between those two lies one of the most important challenges of this century. The consequences of this divide are already visible across critical areas of life. In hiring, artificial intelligence systems evaluate candidates based on patterns derived from historical data, raising concerns about bias and fairness. In privacy, vast amounts of personal data are collected and used in ways individuals may not fully understand. In intellectual property, generative systems challenge traditional definitions of authorship and ownership. In liability, responsibility becomes diffused across multiple actors, making accountability difficult to assign when harm occurs.

At the foundation of all of these issues lies data. Artificial intelligence systems depend on it. Without data, there is no model, and without a model, there is no system. Yet data is also where many of the most significant legal risks begin, including questions of consent, ownership, bias, and permissible use.

Core Principle:
Data is the foundation of artificial intelligence. It is also where legal risk begins.

These challenges are not isolated. They are interconnected. They emerge across the lifecycle of artificial intelligence systems, from data collection to model training to real-world deployment. When these layers are not examined together, risk does not disappear. It compounds.

To understand artificial intelligence in a legal context, it must be viewed not simply as a tool, but as a system of decision making that operates across three interconnected layers. These layers are illustrated below.

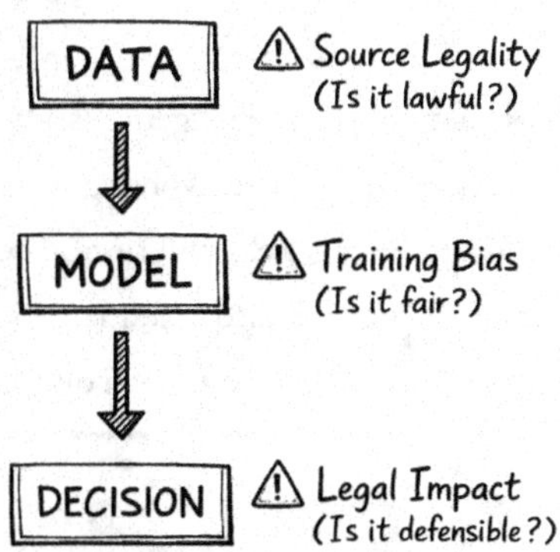

Figure 0.1: AI as a Decision System

At the foundation lies data. This is where patterns originate and where many legal risks begin, including questions of consent, ownership, and bias. Above it sits the model, which transforms data into outputs through statistical learning. At the top sits the decision layer, where those outputs interact with the real world and affect individuals, institutions, and outcomes.

Law does not operate at just one layer. It cuts across all three. It questions how data is collected, how models are trained, and how decisions are applied.

This structure can be reduced to three essential questions:

- Data – Is it lawful?
- Model – Is it fair?
- Decision – Is it defensible?

These questions provide a practical way to evaluate artificial intelligence systems from a legal perspective. They translate technical complexity into legal inquiry. Courts are no longer evaluating isolated pieces of evidence. They are increasingly being asked to evaluate the systems that produce that evidence. Legal analysis is no longer confined to outcomes. It must extend to processes, architectures, and data flows.

This book addresses that transformation directly. It provides a structured framework for understanding artificial intelligence systems, identifying where legal risks emerge, and developing approaches for authentication, challenge, liability, and governance. It equips lawyers with the conceptual tools needed to question AI systems effectively, and it equips technologists with the legal perspective necessary to understand how their systems will be evaluated and trusted.

The central challenge is not that artificial intelligence is advancing too quickly for the law. It is that artificial intelligence and law are evolving alongside each other without sufficient coordination. The future of this field will not be determined solely by breakthroughs in machine learning or by new regulatory frameworks. It will be determined by how effectively law and technology learn to engage with one another.

Principle:

Artificial intelligence will shape decisions. Law will shape the consequences. The gap between them will determine the outcome.

This book is written for those who stand at that intersection.

1

WHY AI AND LAW MUST TALK TO EACH OTHER

The Communication Gap That Is Already Shaping Real-World Decisions

Artificial intelligence is advancing at a pace that challenges not only institutions, but the very frameworks through which society understands responsibility, fairness, and control. Systems that once required human judgment are now being delegated to machines capable of processing vast amounts of data and producing decisions in real time. Yet while the technology moves forward rapidly, the systems designed to regulate it are still catching up.

This misalignment is not simply a matter of speed. It reflects a deeper divide between how technologists and lawyers understand the world, and how each approaches the concept of decision making itself.

Technologists are rewarded for building. Their focus is on innovation, efficiency, and scale. A system that performs well and improves outcomes is considered a success, and progress is often measured by how quickly something can move from concept to application. The culture encourages iteration, experimentation, and rapid deployment, even in environments where the long-term implications are not yet fully understood.

Law operates differently. It is structured around stability, interpretation, and accountability. Legal systems are designed to preserve rights, ensure fairness, and provide remedies when harm occurs. Where technologists seek to optimize systems, lawyers seek to understand and constrain them within defined boundaries.

These are not merely different professional approaches. They are different ways of thinking about risk, responsibility, and control.

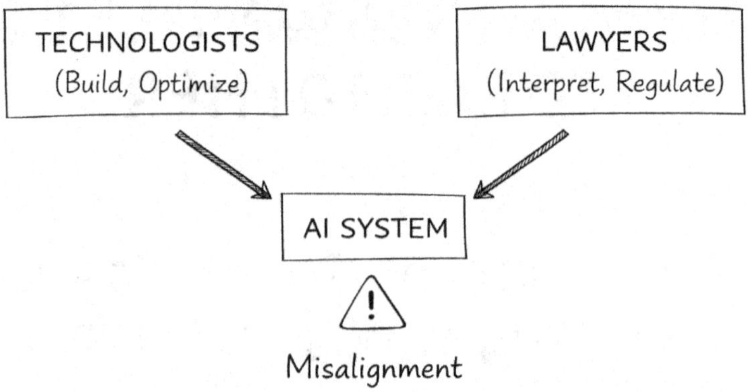

Figure 1.1: The Communication Gap

Technologists speak the language of models, datasets, and optimization. Lawyers speak the language of precedent, liability, and regulation. When these two systems fail to communicate effectively, the result is not just misunderstanding, but the creation of systems that operate without sufficient legal grounding.

> **Key Idea:**
> Artificial intelligence does not exist outside the law. It operates within it, whether the system is designed with that in mind or not.

THE COMMUNICATION GAP

The communication gap between technologists and lawyers is one of the most significant challenges in the development and deployment of artificial intelligence systems. In practice, this gap means that systems are often built without sufficient legal foresight, while legal frameworks are forced to respond only after those systems have already been deployed.

By the time questions of fairness, accountability, or compliance arise, the system is already in operation, sometimes at scale, and in some cases already affecting thousands or millions of individuals.

This creates a reactive cycle in which technology moves first and law follows later. The result is not simply delay, but exposure to risk at a scale that traditional systems were never designed to handle.

At the center of this challenge is a simple but critical reality. Artificial intelligence is not just a technical system. It is a system of decision making, and wherever decisions affect individuals, the law is inevitably involved.

WHY THIS GAP MATTERS

The consequences of this disconnect are already visible across multiple domains. They are not abstract or theoretical. They are practical, widespread, and often difficult to detect in real time.

Artificial intelligence systems are now used in hiring, lending, healthcare, law enforcement, and consumer services. In each of these areas, decisions made by or with the assistance of AI have direct implications for individuals' rights, opportunities, and outcomes.

The issue is not simply that these systems exist. It is how they are built, what they rely on, and how their outputs are used. At the foundation of every AI system is data. Without data, there is no model, and without a model, there is no system.

Central Principle:
Data is the foundation of artificial intelligence, but it is also where legal risk begins.

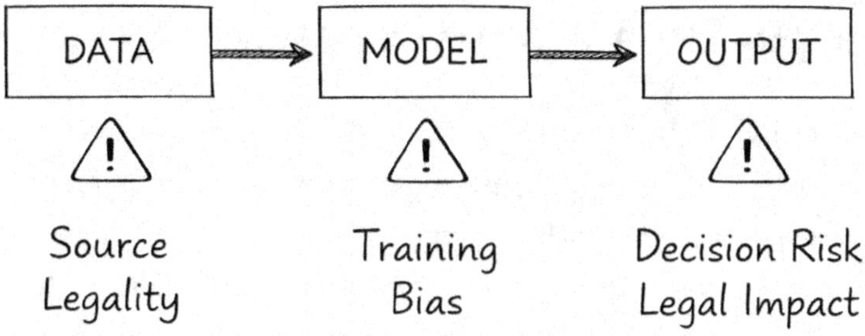

Figure 1.2: Data as the Source of Legal Risk

This dependency on data introduces a wide range of legal questions. What data was used. Who owns that data. Whether consent was obtained. Whether the dataset reflects bias. Whether its use can be justified within existing legal frameworks. These are not peripheral concerns. They are central to how AI systems function and how they should be evaluated.

WHEN SYSTEMS REPRODUCE BIAS

One of the most visible consequences of the communication gap is the persistence of bias within automated systems.

Artificial intelligence systems are trained on historical data, and that data reflects past decisions. Where those decisions contain patterns of inequality, those patterns are learned by the system and reproduced in future outputs unless they are actively identified and corrected.

The controversy surrounding AI-driven hiring systems illustrates this clearly.[1] In systems that analyze facial expressions, speech patterns, and behavioral indicators, concerns have been raised about transparency, consent, and the potential for inherent bias in how candidates are evaluated .

The issue is not simply that such systems exist. It is that individuals being evaluated often do not understand how decisions are being made about them, nor are they in a meaningful position to challenge those decisions.

This is where the legal and technical perspectives begin to diverge. From a technical standpoint, the system may be functioning as designed. From a legal standpoint, the absence of transparency and fairness introduces serious concerns about legitimacy and accountability.

PRIVACY IN THE AGE OF DATA-DRIVEN SYSTEMS

Artificial intelligence systems require large volumes of data to function effectively. This has led to widespread collection, aggregation, and use of personal information, often beyond what individuals reasonably expect.

In ongoing litigation involving major AI developers, plaintiffs have alleged that personal data, including sensitive information, was used to train systems without meaningful

---

1. Jeffrey Dastin, *Amazon Scraps Secret AI Recruiting Tool That Showed Bias Against Women*, Reuters (Oct. 10, 2018).

consent .[2] These claims raise fundamental questions about the boundaries of data use and the extent to which publicly available information can be repurposed for commercial applications.

What makes this issue particularly complex is that individuals often do not know when their data is being used. The harm is not always immediate or visible. It may emerge later, in ways that are difficult to trace back to a specific system or dataset.

Privacy, in this context, is no longer just about access to information. It is about control over how that information is used and the ability to meaningfully consent to that use.

INTELLECTUAL PROPERTY UNDER PRESSURE

Generative artificial intelligence has introduced a new set of challenges for intellectual property law. Systems capable of generating images, text, and other creative outputs are trained on vast collections of existing works. These systems do not copy in a traditional sense, but they learn from patterns derived from those works in ways that challenge established legal definitions.

Legal disputes involving artists, authors, and technology companies have already begun to test these boundaries. Claims have been made that copyrighted works were used without permission to train systems that can now generate similar outputs at scale.[3] These cases are forcing courts to confront a fundamental question. What does it mean, in legal terms, for a system to learn from a work, and where should the boundary be drawn between learning and infringement.

ACCOUNTABILITY IN COMPLEX SYSTEMS

One of the most challenging issues in artificial intelligence is determining responsibility when something goes wrong. Traditional legal frameworks are built around identifiable

---

2. *The New York Times Co. v. Microsoft Corp. and OpenAI*, No. 1:23-cv-11195 (S.D.N .Y. filed Dec. 27, 2023); see also Reuters, *OpenAI Fights Order to Turn Over Millions of ChatGPT Conversations* (2025).

3. *Andersen v. Stability AI Ltd.*, No. 3:23-cv-00201 (N.D. Cal. 2023); *Getty Images v. Stability AI*, pending litigation in the United Kingdom and United States

actors and linear processes. A product is designed, manufactured, and used. When harm occurs, responsibility can often be traced through that chain.

Artificial intelligence complicates this structure. A system may be developed by one entity, trained on data from another, deployed by a third, and used by a fourth. When harm occurs, responsibility is distributed across multiple actors, making accountability difficult to assign.

Figure 1.3: Diffusion of Responsibility

This challenge is evident in cases involving automated decision systems. In one instance, an automated system used to detect unemployment fraud incorrectly flagged thousands of individuals, leading to significant financial and personal harm.[4] The issue was not simply technical failure. It was the absence of meaningful oversight and mechanisms for correction.

> Critical Observation:
> When decision making is automated, responsibility does not disappear. It becomes harder to locate.

TRANSPARENCY, FAIRNESS, AND TRUST

For artificial intelligence systems to function effectively within society, they must be trusted. Trust, however, is not built through performance alone. It is built through transparency, fairness, and accountability.

Legal systems emphasize these principles because they provide a framework through which decisions can be evaluated, challenged, and, where necessary, corrected. Artificial

---

4. Michigan's automated unemployment fraud detection system, commonly referred to as the MiDAS controversy, incorrectly accused thousands of individuals of fraud between 2013 and 2015.

intelligence systems, particularly those operating as black boxes, often struggle to meet these expectations.

Courts and regulators are increasingly focusing on whether individuals are given sufficient notice, whether decisions can be explained, and whether there are mechanisms for review. These are not optional features. They are legal requirements that determine whether a system can operate legitimately within society.

BRIDGING THE GAP

The communication gap between technologists and lawyers is not inevitable. It can be addressed, but doing so requires a shift in approach on both sides.

Lawyers must engage earlier in the development process, not only at the point of dispute. This requires an understanding of how systems function, what data they rely on, and where risks are likely to emerge. It does not require technical specialization, but it does require conceptual clarity.

Technologists must also expand their perspective. Building systems that perform well is no longer sufficient. Systems must be designed with legal and societal implications in mind from the outset, rather than addressed after deployment.

Earlier collaboration between technologists and legal professionals is therefore essential. Legal risks should be examined before systems are deployed, not only after harm occurs. Lawyers must become more proactive, while technologists must incorporate legal analysis into the design stage of system development.

> **Central Principle:**
> Responsible artificial intelligence is not achieved after deployment. It is built into the system from the beginning.

As artificial intelligence becomes more deeply embedded in everyday decision making, the cost of misalignment between law and technology becomes increasingly expensive. What begins as a technical design choice can evolve into a legal issue, and what appears to be a legal question may originate in the architecture of the system itself.

The future of this field will not be determined solely by advances in machine learning or by the introduction of new regulatory frameworks. It will be shaped by how effectively these two domains learn to engage with one another, not as separate disciplines, but as parts of a shared system.

Closing Principle:

Artificial intelligence will shape decisions. Law will shape the consequences. The strength of the connection between them will determine the outcome.

2

AI FUNDAMENTALS FOR LAWYERS

How AI Works Without Technical Overwhelm

The practice of law is undergoing a structural transformation driven by artificial intelligence. Tasks that once required extensive human effort, including document review, contract analysis, and legal research, are increasingly being augmented or partially automated by AI systems.[1] What was once considered experimental has now become part of mainstream legal practice.

Despite this shift, many lawyers remain hesitant to engage with artificial intelligence. This hesitation is not rooted in resistance to innovation, but in the complexity and technical language that often surrounds it. Terms such as machine learning, large language models, and neural networks can appear inaccessible, creating the impression that meaningful engagement requires deep technical expertise.

That impression is misleading. Lawyers do not need to become engineers, but they do need a working understanding of how these systems function. AI literacy is not about

1. Richard Susskind, *Tomorrow's Lawyers: An Introduction to Your Future* (2d ed. 2017); American Bar Association, *Generative AI and the Practice of Law* (2024).

coding. It is about comprehension. It allows lawyers to ask informed questions, identify legal risks, and use AI tools effectively without compromising professional responsibility.

Without that level of understanding, the risk extends beyond inefficiency. Lawyers may rely on systems that appear authoritative while producing outputs that are incomplete, biased, or incorrect.

DEMYSTIFYING ARTIFICIAL INTELLIGENCE

At its core, artificial intelligence is not magic. It is pattern recognition at scale. AI systems analyze large volumes of data, identify patterns within that data, and use those patterns to make predictions or generate outputs.

> **Core Principle:**
> Artificial intelligence does not understand. It predicts.

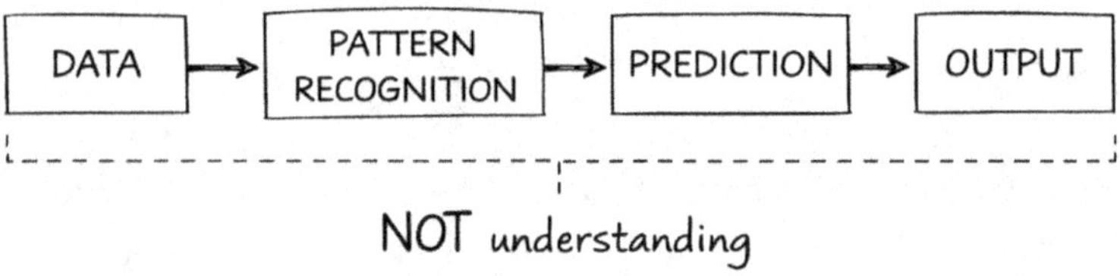

Figure 2.1: What AI Actually Does

Machine learning enables systems to improve performance over time by learning from data. A model trained on thousands of contracts can identify patterns, detect anomalies, and flag unusual provisions. Natural language processing allows systems to interpret and generate human language, powering tools used in legal drafting, research, and review.

Generative AI extends this capability further by producing new content. Large language models generate text that is often coherent and persuasive. However, coherence is not the same as accuracy. These systems rely on probability, not reasoning, which means they can produce outputs that sound correct while being entirely wrong.

AI THROUGH A LEGAL LENS

To understand artificial intelligence from a legal perspective, one principle must be clear.

Core Principle:
Data is to artificial intelligence what blood is to the human body.

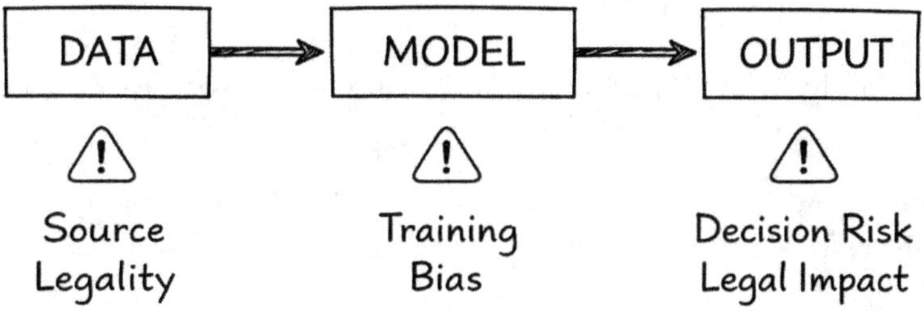

Figure 2.2: AI Through a Legal Lens

Every AI system depends on data. Without data, there is no model, and without a model, there is no output. This dependency introduces immediate legal implications.

Lawyers must consider the source of the data, whether consent was obtained, whether the dataset reflects bias, and whether its use complies with applicable legal standards. These questions arise not only when disputes occur, but at the point where systems are designed and deployed.

Practical Check

Before trusting any AI output, ask:

- Where did the data come from?
- Was consent obtained?
- Could this dataset contain bias?
- Would this use withstand legal scrutiny?

Legal issues linked to artificial intelligence extend across intellectual property, privacy, discrimination, transparency, and liability. Each of these areas is engaged the moment an AI system is used in a real-world context.

WHEN AI ENTERS LEGAL PRACTICE

The need for AI literacy becomes evident when examining how these tools are already being used.

In one widely discussed incident, attorneys relied on an AI-generated legal brief that included fabricated case citations.[2] The citations appeared credible but did not exist. The court imposed sanctions and made it clear that reliance on AI does not remove the lawyer's responsibility to verify accuracy.

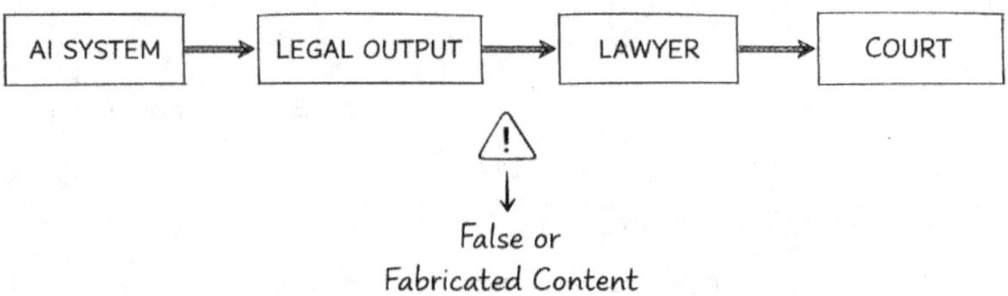

Figure 2.3: AI Risk in Legal Practice

> **Lawyer's Note:**
> The use of AI in drafting does not diminish the lawyer's duty to verify accuracy and reliability. Any content that cannot be independently validated should not be submitted.

At the same time, artificial intelligence is delivering measurable value in legal practice. In contract review, AI systems can analyze thousands of agreements in seconds, extracting key clauses and identifying risks. In litigation, predictive coding allows lawyers to identify relevant documents quickly, significantly reducing time and cost.

These tools are not replacing lawyers. They are changing how legal work is performed, and if utilized properly, they can improve lawyers' efficiency.

RISKS LAWYERS CANNOT IGNORE

The integration of artificial intelligence into legal workflows introduces new categories of risk that cannot be overlooked.

One of the most significant risks is the generation of false information that appears credible. AI systems may produce outputs that are plausible but incorrect, and the authoritative manner in which these outputs are presented can make errors difficult to detect.[3]

Bias presents another challenge. Because AI systems learn from historical data, they may reproduce existing inequalities embedded within that data. This has been observed in hiring technologies, where algorithmic decision making can reflect and reinforce systemic bias.[4]

Confidentiality is equally critical. Inputting sensitive client information into AI systems, particularly public tools, may expose that information in ways that conflict with professional obligations.

Practical Check

Before using AI in legal work, consider:

- Does this involve confidential client data?
- Can this output be independently verified?
- Could this result introduce bias or unfair outcomes?

Professional competence now includes understanding these risks. Lawyers are expected not only to use technology, but to understand its implications.

3. OpenAI, *GPT-4 Technical Report* (2023).

4. Jeffrey Dastin, *Amazon Scraps Secret AI Recruiting Tool That Showed Bias Against Women*, Reuters (Oct. 10, 2018).

THE LAWYER'S APPROACH TO AI

Artificial intelligence should be approached with balance. It is neither something to be avoided nor something to be blindly trusted.

> **Core Principle:**
> AI is a tool, not a decision maker.

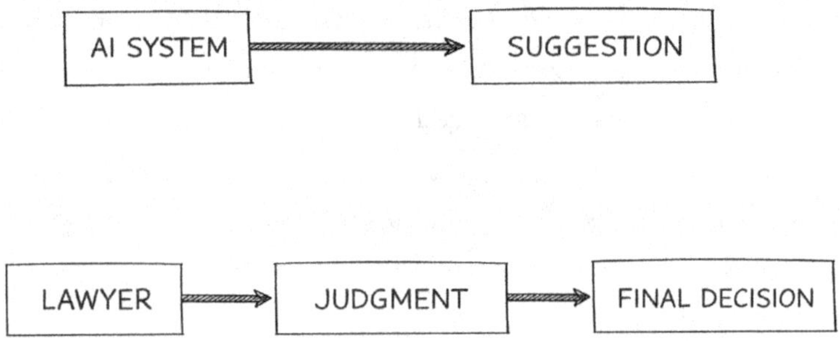

Figure 2.4: The Lawyer's Role vs AI

The role of the lawyer remains unchanged at its core. Judgment, accountability, and ethical responsibility cannot be delegated to a system. AI can enhance efficiency, reveal patterns, and support decision making. However, it cannot replace the reasoning required to interpret law, apply it to facts, and act in the best interest of a client.

To wrap up this chapter, Artificial intelligence is already embedded in legal practice. Its influence will continue to expand, shaping how work is performed and how decisions are made. The defining difference will not be access to AI, but understanding of it.

Lawyers who develop AI literacy will be able to use these tools effectively while maintaining professional standards. Those who do not may rely on systems they do not fully understand, exposing themselves and their clients to unnecessary risk. The future of law will not be determined by artificial intelligence alone. It will be shaped by how lawyers choose to engage with it.

3

LEGAL FOUNDATIONS FOR AI PROFESSIONALS

What Technologists Must Know to Avoid Legal Risk

Artificial intelligence is not built in a vacuum. Every system that is designed, trained, and deployed operates within a legal environment, whether acknowledged or not. For AI professionals, the focus is often on performance, scalability, and innovation. However, systems that are technically sound can still fail when they are legally flawed. Legal awareness is no longer optional. It is part of responsible system design.

Developers, data scientists, and product managers are not expected to function as lawyers. What is required, however, is the ability to recognize when legal risks are present, understand the implications of design choices, and know when to involve legal expertise. Systems that ignore legal constraints often face consequences that extend beyond regulatory penalties. They risk reputational damage, product failure, and loss of user trust. At the center of this intersection is a simple but powerful idea.

Core Principle:
Data is to artificial intelligence what blood is to the human body.

Every AI system is built on data. The legality of that system is therefore inseparable from the legality of the data that powers it.

THE LEGAL LAYERS OF AI DEVELOPMENT

Legal risk in AI does not arise at a single point. It exists across the lifecycle of a system, from data collection to deployment and real-world use.

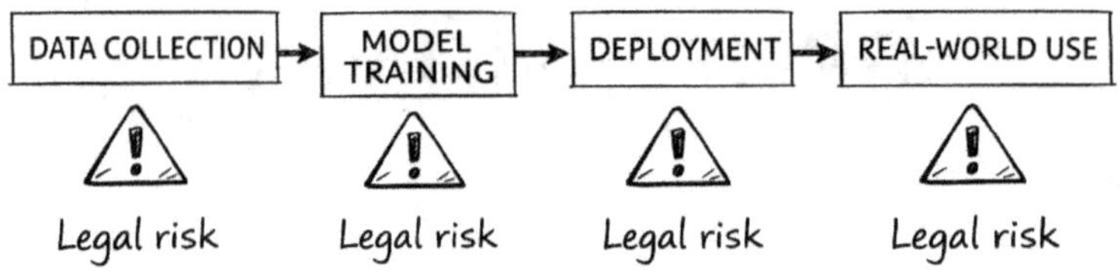

Figure 3.1: Legal Risk Across the AI Lifecycle

A useful way to understand this is through three recurring questions that apply at every stage of development:

Practical Check

Before building or deploying an AI system, ask:

- What data is being used and where did it come from?
- Do we have the legal right to use this data?
- What are the foreseeable consequences of this system's decisions?

These questions appear simple, but they sit at the heart of nearly every legal dispute involving artificial intelligence.

DATA PRIVACY: THE FIRST LINE OF DEFENSE

Artificial intelligence depends on large volumes of data, much of which may include personal or sensitive information. Privacy law exists to define the boundaries of how that data can be collected, processed, and used.

In practice, privacy violations often arise not from malicious intent, but from assumptions. The assumption that publicly available data is free to use. The assumption that scale justifies collection. The assumption that users understand how their data is being used. These assumptions are frequently incorrect.

In the European Union, the General Data Protection Regulation establishes strict requirements around consent, transparency, and purpose limitation.[1] Organizations must clearly explain how data is used and ensure that processing aligns with the purpose for which the data was collected. Noncompliance carries significant financial penalties.

In the United States, privacy regulation is more fragmented, but no less significant. Laws governing health data, education data, children's data, and consumer privacy impose specific obligations depending on the type of information involved. State-level frameworks such as California's consumer privacy laws further expand these requirements.[2]

Legal disputes have already begun to test the boundaries of data use in AI systems. In one case involving AI developers, plaintiffs alleged that personal data, including information relating to minors, was used without consent to train AI models.[3] These claims highlight a growing concern that data collection practices may exceed what users reasonably expect or authorize.

Technologist's Note:
Publicly available does not mean legally usable.

For AI professionals, privacy compliance must be embedded at the design stage. Retrofitting compliance after deployment is often ineffective and costly.

INTELLECTUAL PROPERTY: INNOVATION WITHIN BOUNDARIES

AI development raises fundamental questions about ownership, authorship, and the use of existing works. Training data is often at the center of these disputes. Large-scale AI systems rely on datasets that may include copyrighted materials such as books, images, and music. When these materials are used without permission, legal challenges can arise.

---

1. Regulation (EU) 2016/679 (General Data Protection Regulation) (GDPR).

2. California Consumer Privacy Act (CCPA), Cal. Civ. Code § 1798.100 et seq.

3. *M. v. OpenAI LP*, No. 3:23-cv-03199 (N.D. Cal. filed June 28, 2023).

Ongoing litigation has made this issue unavoidable. In cases involving image generation systems, artists have argued that their works were used without authorization to train models capable of reproducing their styles.[4] Courts have allowed certain claims to proceed, signaling that the legal system is taking these concerns seriously.

Similarly, claims brought by authors against AI developers focus on the use of entire copyrighted works in training large language models.[5] The argument is not simply about copying, but about whether the commercial value of these systems is built on unauthorized use of protected material.

Questions also arise regarding outputs generated by AI systems. In many jurisdictions, copyright protection requires human authorship.[6] This means that fully AI-generated works may not qualify for protection unless there is sufficient human creative contribution.

Core Principle:
If humans are not meaningfully involved, legal protection becomes uncertain.

Trade secrets introduce another layer of complexity. Companies often treat their models, datasets, and processes as proprietary. However, increasing demands for transparency, particularly in high-risk systems, can conflict with claims of secrecy.

For technologists, the implication is clear. Innovation must operate within legal boundaries. Using data without permission or failing to account for ownership can undermine the very systems being built.

---

4. *Andersen v. Stability AI Ltd.*, No. 3:23-cv-00201 (N.D. Cal. 2023).

5. *Authors Guild v. OpenAI*, pending litigation concerning the use of copyrighted books in training large language models.

6. *Thaler v. Perlmutter*, 687 F. Supp. 3d 140 (D.D.C. 2023); U.S. Copyright Office, *Copyright Registration Guidance: Works Containing Material Generated by Artificial Intelligence* (2023).

DISCRIMINATION AND BIAS: WHEN SYSTEMS INHERIT INEQUALITY

Artificial intelligence systems learn from historical data. When that data reflects existing inequalities, those inequalities can be reproduced and amplified.

The law does not require intent for liability to arise. Outcomes are often what matter. In employment contexts, legal frameworks prohibit discrimination on the basis of protected characteristics.[7] If an AI system disproportionately excludes certain groups, even without deliberate intent, liability can follow.

This concern is not theoretical. In a well-known regulatory complaint involving an AI hiring platform, the use of biometric and behavioral analysis raised questions about fairness, transparency, and potential bias.[8] The system analyzed facial expressions and speech patterns to assess candidates, leading to concerns that such methods could disadvantage certain groups and operate without meaningful consent.

The outcome of that scrutiny led to changes in how the technology was used, including the discontinuation of certain features.

Practical Check

When evaluating an AI system, ask:

- Is the training data representative and balanced?
- Could this system produce unequal outcomes across groups?
- Can the decision-making process be explained?

Bias in AI is not only a technical issue. It is a legal and ethical one.

---

7. Title VII of the Civil Rights Act of 1964, 42 U.S.C. § 2000e et seq.

8. Electronic Privacy Information Center (EPIC), FTC Complaint Regarding HireVue's AI Hiring Assessments (2019).

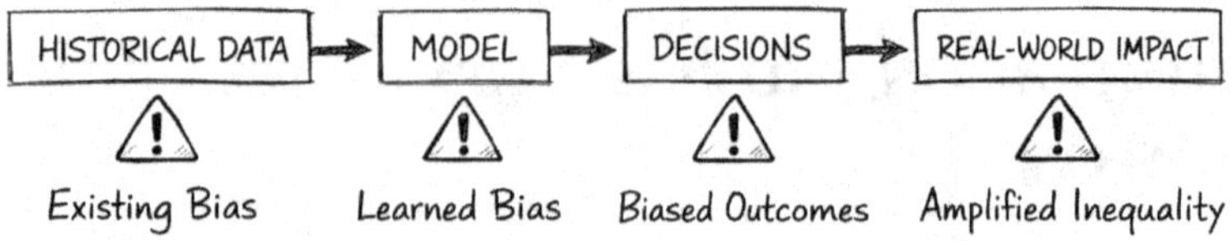

Figure 3.2: Bias Propagation in AI Systems

TRANSPARENCY, ACCOUNTABILITY, AND THE "BLACK BOX" PROBLEM

One of the defining challenges of modern AI systems is their opacity. Complex models can produce decisions that are difficult to interpret, even by their developers. This lack of transparency creates legal risk.

Users affected by AI-driven decisions may not understand how those decisions were made. In high-stakes contexts such as healthcare, employment, or public benefits, this lack of clarity can undermine trust and raise due process concerns.

Legal disputes have already illustrated these risks. In cases involving automated decision systems used by government agencies, individuals were subjected to penalties or reduced benefits based on algorithmic determinations that lacked adequate explanation or human oversight.[9] Error rates in such systems were significant, leading to widespread harm.

> **Core Principle:**
> If a system cannot be explained, it becomes difficult to justify.

Transparency does not require revealing proprietary code. It requires providing meaningful information about how decisions are made and ensuring that those decisions can be challenged when necessary.

9. Michigan's MiDAS automated fraud detection system incorrectly accused thousands of unemployment fraud between 2013 and 2015.

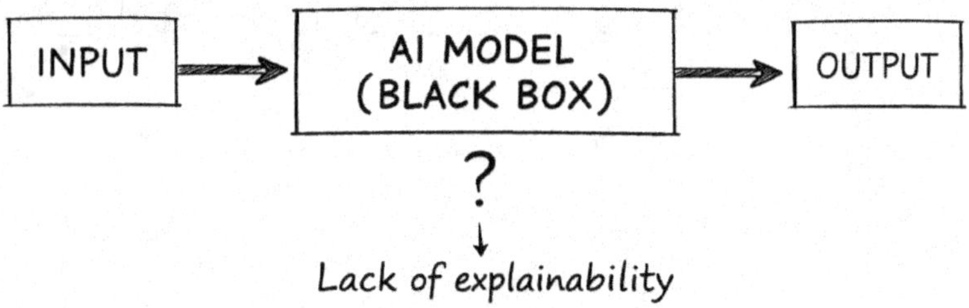

Figure 3.3: The Black Box Problem

NEGLIGENCE AND LIABILITY: WHEN SYSTEMS CAUSE HARM

AI systems are not immune from traditional legal principles. When harm occurs, questions of responsibility arise. Developers and companies owe a duty of care to those affected by their systems, extending across the lifecycle of a product from design to deployment and operation. However, liability is not fixed and may, in certain circumstances, shift to users, particularly where harm results from misuse, improper application, or a failure to independently verify outputs

Failures can occur in multiple ways. A system may be defectively designed. Risks may not be adequately tested. Known issues may not be disclosed. In cases involving autonomous systems, plaintiffs have argued that companies failed to ensure compliance with safety standards, resulting in injury.[10] These claims are grounded in established legal principles of negligence and product liability.

Lawyer's Note:
Innovation does not eliminate responsibility.

AI may introduce new forms of risk, but it does not remove existing legal obligations.

10. Product liability and negligence claims involving autonomous driving systems have emerged in litigation concerning Tesla Autopilot and similar technologies.

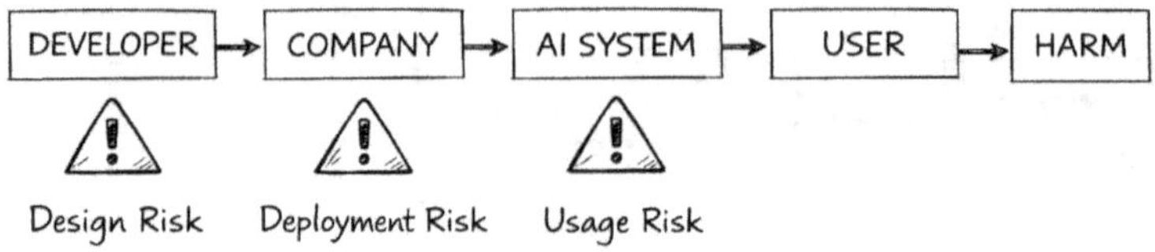

Figure 3.4: Liability Chain

THE GLOBAL DIMENSION: WHEN AI CROSSES BORDERS

Artificial intelligence systems often operate across jurisdictions. Data may be collected in one country, processed in another, and deployed globally. This creates complex legal questions about which laws apply and how conflicts between legal systems should be resolved.

As AI adoption increases, cross-border legal issues will become more prominent. Technologists must be aware that compliance in one jurisdiction does not guarantee compliance in another.

A PRACTICAL WAY FORWARD

Legal literacy for AI professionals is not about memorizing statutes or becoming experts in regulatory frameworks. It is about developing the ability to recognize risk and act responsibly.

Practical Check

Before launching any AI system, consider:

- Have legal risks been identified at each stage of development?
- Has sensitive data been handled in compliance with applicable laws?
- Are the system's outputs reliable, explainable, and fair?

These questions do not slow innovation. They strengthen it.

Another practical step is early collaboration. Technologists should engage with legal professionals at the earliest stages of system design, before an AI system is built or deployed. Identifying legal and regulatory risks at this stage is often more effective than attempting to address them after development is complete.

Artificial intelligence is reshaping industries, including law itself. The systems being developed today will influence decisions, opportunities, and outcomes at scale. Responsibility for these systems does not rest solely with lawyers or regulators. It also lies with the professionals who design and deploy them.

The most effective AI professionals will not only understand how to build systems. They will also understand the legal and societal context in which those systems operate. That understanding is what separates innovation that succeeds from innovation that fails.

4

ALGORITHMIC BIAS AND CIVIL RIGHTS

How AI Can Reinforce Inequality and How to Recognize It

Artificial intelligence is often described as objective, data-driven, and neutral. The assumption is that removing human judgment from decision making eliminates bias. Experience has shown that this assumption is flawed, because AI systems do not remove bias but learn from data, and when that data reflects historical inequality, those patterns are reproduced and often amplified.

Bias in artificial intelligence is therefore not accidental. It is structural, embedded in the way systems are built and trained.

To understand this, it is necessary to begin with how the law defines discrimination. Legal systems traditionally recognize both intentional discrimination and outcomes that disproportionately harm protected groups.[1] Artificial intelligence complicates this distinction because most systems are not explicitly programmed to discriminate, yet they can produce outcomes that closely resemble unlawful bias.

1. Title VII of the Civil Rights Act of 1964, 42 U.S.C. § 2000e et seq.; *Griggs v. Duke Power Co.*, 401 U.S. 424 (1971).

Core Principle:
AI reflects the past. If the past is unequal, the output will be unequal.

A WORKING MENTAL MODEL FOR ALGORITHMIC BIAS

Understanding algorithmic bias requires moving beyond definitions and adopting a structured way of thinking. Bias does not appear suddenly at the point of decision. It is introduced, shaped, and reinforced across stages of a system's lifecycle.

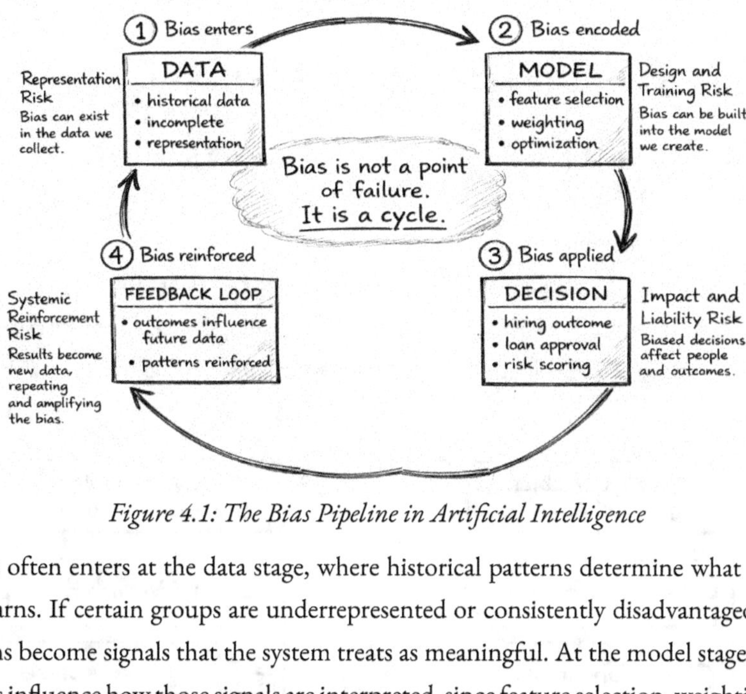

Figure 4.1: The Bias Pipeline in Artificial Intelligence

Bias often enters at the data stage, where historical patterns determine what the system learns. If certain groups are underrepresented or consistently disadvantaged, those patterns become signals that the system treats as meaningful. At the model stage, design choices influence how those signals are interpreted, since feature selection, weighting, and optimization goals all shape outcomes.

At the decision stage, the system applies learned patterns to real-world situations, often at scale and without visibility. The feedback loop then reinforces the system, because decisions generated by the model may influence future data, creating a cycle where bias is not only repeated but strengthened over time.

Practical Check

When assessing any AI system, consider:

- What historical patterns are embedded in the data?
- How the model might amplify those patterns?
- Whether outcomes differ across groups?
- Whether the system learns from its own outputs?

THE PROXY PROBLEM: HOW BIAS HIDES

One of the most complex aspects of algorithmic bias is that it is rarely explicit. Even when protected characteristics such as race or gender are removed, systems can rely on proxy variables that carry similar information.

Location data, educational background, purchasing behavior, and language patterns can all serve as indirect indicators. As a result, a system can produce discriminatory outcomes without ever explicitly using prohibited variables, which makes bias harder to detect and address.

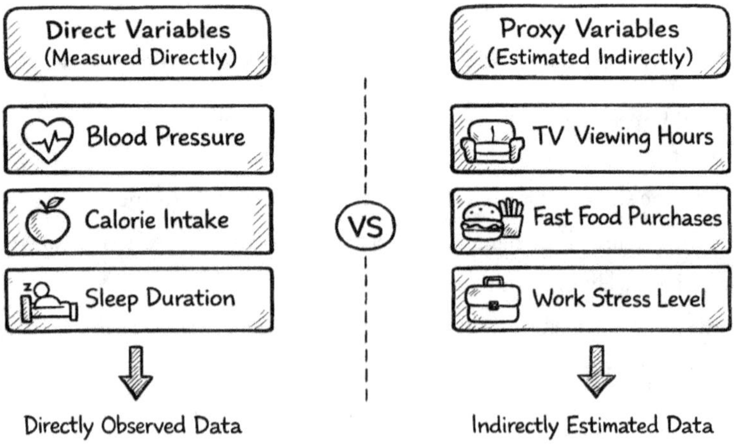

Figure 4.2: Direct Variables vs Proxy Variables

Core Principle:
Removing sensitive attributes does not remove bias. It often conceals it.

This is why purely technical fixes are insufficient, because bias is not only a coding problem but a structural issue that requires both technical and legal awareness.

WHEN SCALE CHANGES EVERYTHING

In traditional decision making, bias operates at the level of individuals. A biased recruiter may affect a limited number of applicants, and a biased lending officer may influence a series of decisions within a constrained environment.

Artificial intelligence changes this completely because once a pattern is embedded in a model, it is applied consistently across a large number of cases. This transforms isolated bias into systemic outcomes that can affect entire populations.

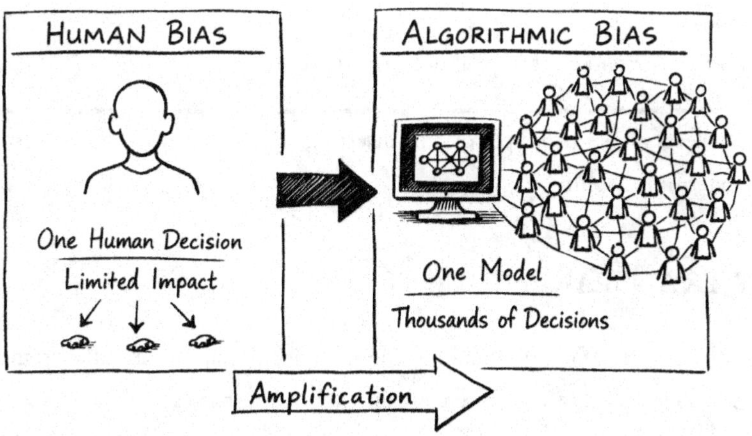

Figure 4.3: Human Bias vs Algorithmic Bias

Core Principle:
Scale turns bias into infrastructure.

The significance of this shift is not only the number of decisions affected, but the consistency with which those decisions are applied, often without visibility or intervention.

CASE ANALYSIS: AUTOMATED HIRING SYSTEMS

The impact of algorithmic bias becomes clearer when examined through real-world systems. In hiring, AI tools are often used to screen candidates, rank résumés, and assess suitability, and these systems rely heavily on historical data.

Where past hiring practices reflect imbalance, the system learns those patterns and begins to favor candidates who resemble previously successful hires. This does not occur because the system is intentionally discriminatory, but because it optimizes for patterns it has been trained to recognize.

Legal challenges have emerged where applicants allege that automated systems function as barriers rather than neutral evaluators. In such cases, the issue is not only technical accuracy but whether the system produces outcomes that disproportionately exclude certain groups.

> **Lawyer's Note:**
> A neutral system can still produce unlawful outcomes.

This reflects a core principle of anti-discrimination law, where outcomes, not just intent, determine liability.

WHY TRANSPARENCY MATTERS

One of the central difficulties in addressing algorithmic bias is the lack of transparency. Many AI systems operate in ways that are difficult to interpret, and their decision-making processes may be embedded within complex structures that do not provide clear explanations.

This creates a problem for legal accountability because individuals affected by AI-driven decisions may not understand how those decisions were made. Without that understanding, it becomes difficult to challenge outcomes or identify whether bias is present.

Figure 4.4: The Black Box Problem

> **Core Principle:**
> If a decision cannot be explained, it becomes difficult to justify.

Transparency does not require revealing proprietary systems in full detail, but it does require providing meaningful explanations and ensuring that decisions can be reviewed and challenged.

LEGAL RESPONSES AND EMERGING STANDARDS

Legal systems are beginning to respond to the challenges posed by algorithmic bias. Existing civil rights laws continue to apply, and organizations remain responsible for the outcomes of the tools they use, regardless of whether those tools are automated.

At the same time, new approaches are emerging, particularly in areas where AI systems have significant impact. Requirements such as bias audits, documentation, and testing are increasingly being introduced to ensure that systems are evaluated before deployment.

Globally, regulatory frameworks are evolving to classify certain AI systems as high risk, subjecting them to stricter oversight and accountability measures[2]. These developments signal a shift toward proactive governance rather than reactive enforcement.

2. European Union Artificial Intelligence Act (EU AI Act).

THE LIMITS OF CURRENT LEGAL FRAMEWORKS

Despite these developments, challenges remain. Traditional legal approaches often rely on identifying intent or demonstrating statistical disparity, but AI systems complicate both because their internal logic may not be easily accessible or interpretable.[3]

This creates a gap between harm and proof, where individuals may experience adverse outcomes without being able to demonstrate how or why those outcomes occurred.[4]

To address this challenge, proposals have emerged that emphasize greater transparency, stronger documentation requirements, and the use of impact assessments before systems are deployed. These approaches aim to shift attention toward prevention rather than remediation.

A UNIFIED WAY TO THINK ABOUT BIAS

To bring these ideas together, it is useful to think of algorithmic bias as a system rather than a single event.

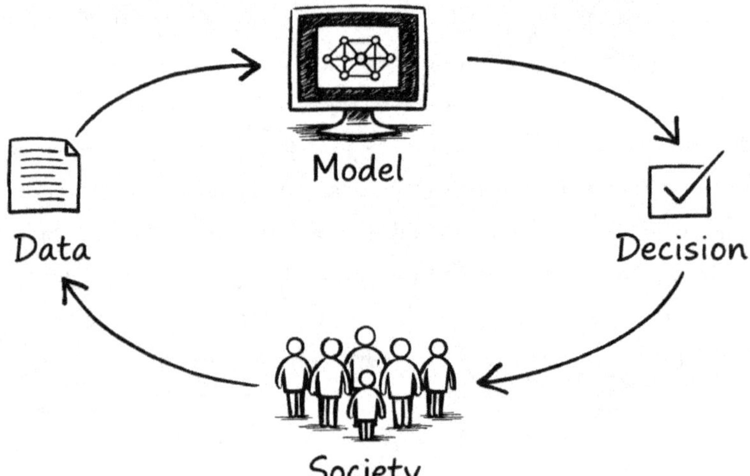

Figure 4.5: The Bias System

---

3. *Washington v. Davis*, 426 U.S. 229 (1976).

4. Frank Pasquale, *The Black Box Society* (2015).

Bias enters through data, is shaped by the model, influences decisions, and then feeds back into society, where new data is generated. This cycle allows bias to persist and, in some cases, intensify over time.

Core Principle:
Bias in AI is not an event. It is a system that reinforces itself.

As a final reflection, algorithmic bias represents one of the most significant challenges at the intersection of artificial intelligence and law. It sits at the point where technical design meets legal responsibility and societal impact, requiring both disciplines to engage with the problem in a coordinated way.

Artificial intelligence does not operate outside the law, and the systems being built today will shape access to opportunities, resources, and outcomes at scale. The question is not whether bias can exist in these systems, but whether it is recognized, measured, and addressed in a way that aligns with legal and ethical standards.

The future of fair and accountable AI will depend on how effectively technologists and legal professionals work together to understand and manage this risk.

5

AI AND PRIVACY LAW

How Data Is Used, Controlled, and Exposed in AI Systems

Artificial intelligence does not begin with algorithms. It begins with data. Every system, regardless of its complexity, is shaped by the information it consumes. Without data, there is no learning, no pattern recognition, and no output. In this sense, data is not simply an input into artificial intelligence systems. It is their foundation, their structure, and their limit .

This dependency creates a fundamental legal tension. The same data that enables innovation also creates exposure. The more data a system ingests, the more powerful it becomes, but also the more intrusive it can be. What appears as technical advancement is often built on large-scale data collection, aggregation, and reuse, frequently beyond the awareness of the individuals whose information is involved.

Privacy law exists to define the boundaries of that process. It asks questions that technology alone cannot answer. What data can be collected. Under what conditions. For what purpose. And for how long. Artificial intelligence has not eliminated these questions. It has intensified them.

A STRUCTURAL WAY TO THINK ABOUT PRIVACY IN AI

Privacy in artificial intelligence is often discussed in fragmented terms, focusing on consent, compliance, or regulation. A more useful way to understand it is as a system.

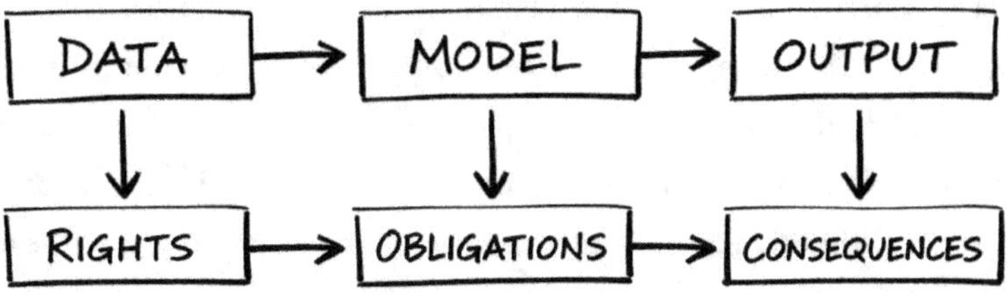

Figure 5.1: The Data Power and Risk Model

This model reflects a simple but powerful idea. Every technical stage has a legal counterpart.

At the data stage, the law is concerned with rights. Individuals have interests in how their data is collected, whether consent was obtained, and whether the source of the data is legitimate. At the model stage, the focus shifts to obligations. Organizations must ensure that data is used within lawful boundaries, that processing is limited to defined and authorized purposes, and that safeguards are in place.

At the output stage, consequences emerge. Decisions made by AI systems affect individuals, sometimes in ways that are difficult to reverse. The legal system evaluates these outcomes, not only in terms of harm, but also in terms of accountability.

> **Core Principle:**
> Every AI system is also a legal system in operation.

THE COLLAPSE OF TRADITIONAL CONSENT

Consent has long been treated as the foundation of privacy law.[1] It assumes that individuals understand what they are agreeing to and can make informed choices about how their data is used. Artificial intelligence challenges this assumption at every level.

Data used in AI systems is rarely collected for a single purpose. It is aggregated, combined, and repurposed. Information provided in one context may later be used in another, often far removed from the original interaction. Individuals may consent to the use of a service without understanding that their data could contribute to the training of large-scale models.

Legal disputes have begun to expose this gap. In *T. v. OpenAI LP*, plaintiffs alleged that personal information, including that of minors, was used without meaningful consent to train AI systems.[2] The significance of such claims lies not only in the specific facts, but in what they reveal about the limits of existing consent models.

Consent is no longer a discrete event. It is an evolving condition that must account for how data is reused over time.

> **Critical Observation:**
> Consent without understanding is not meaningful consent.

DATA SCALE AND THE PROBLEM OF INVISIBILITY

One of the defining characteristics of modern AI systems is scale. Data is collected from multiple sources, processed across distributed systems, and embedded into models in ways that are not easily observable.

---

1. Alan F. Westin, *Privacy and Freedom* (1967); Regulation (EU) 2016/679 (General Data Protection Regulation).

2. *T. v. OpenAI LP*, litigation alleging unauthorized use of personal information, including data relating to minors, in AI training datasets.

This creates a condition of invisibility.[3] Individuals often do not know what data has been collected about them, how it has been used, or whether it has influenced decisions that affect them.

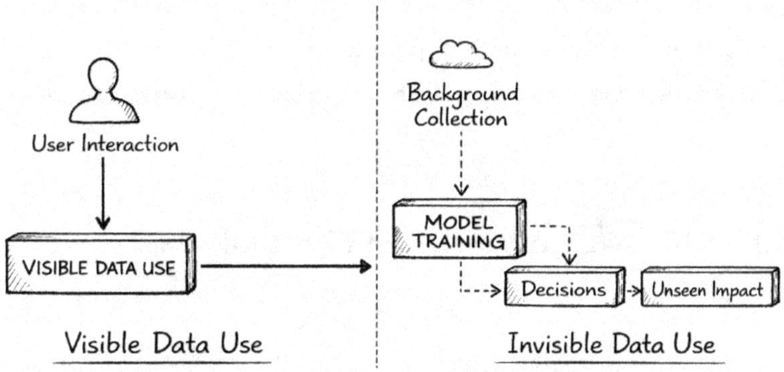

Figure 5.2: Visible vs Invisible Data Use

This invisibility creates a challenge for both law and governance. Rights that cannot be exercised, and harms that cannot be identified, are difficult to regulate.

> **Core Principle:**
> What cannot be seen cannot be easily challenged.

REGULATORY RESPONSES: TWO DIFFERENT PHILOSOPHIES

Legal systems have responded to these challenges in different ways.

The European approach, reflected in comprehensive frameworks, emphasizes structure. It establishes clear rules around data collection, processing, and individual rights. It also places limits on automated decision making, particularly where such decisions have significant effects on individuals.[4]

---

3. Frank Pasquale, *The Black Box Society* (2015).

4. Regulation (EU) 2016/679 (General Data Protection Regulation); Regulation (EU) 2024/1689 (Artificial Intelligence Act). [1, 2]

The United States, by contrast, follows a more fragmented approach.[5] Privacy protections are distributed across multiple laws, each addressing specific types of data or contexts. This creates flexibility, but also inconsistency.

The difference between these approaches is not merely technical. It reflects two distinct philosophies. One prioritizes uniform protection. The other adapts to context. Both approaches are now being tested by artificial intelligence systems that operate across jurisdictions and at global scale.

BIOMETRIC DATA AND IRREVERSIBLE RISK

Not all data carries the same level of risk. Biometric data occupies a distinct category because it is inherently tied to identity.

Facial images, fingerprints, and voice patterns cannot be changed once compromised.[6] Their use in AI systems raises concerns that extend beyond traditional privacy frameworks. When biometric data is collected and used without clear boundaries, the consequences are not easily reversed. Systems that rely on such data may continue to operate long after individuals have lost control over their information.

> **Core Principle:**
> The more permanent the data, the greater the legal risk.

SURVEILLANCE AS INFRASTRUCTURE

Artificial intelligence has transformed surveillance from a targeted activity into an infrastructure. Systems can continuously collect, analyze, and interpret data about individuals and groups. This shift has implications that go beyond privacy. It affects autonomy,

---

5. California Consumer Privacy Act (CCPA), Cal. Civ. Code § 1798.100 et seq.; Health Insurance Portability and Accountability Act (HIPAA), 42 U.S.C. § 1320d et seq.

6. Illinois Biometric Information Privacy Act (BIPA), 740 ILCS 14/1 *et seq.*; *see also* Woodrow Hartzog, *Privacy's Blueprint* (2018) (discussing the unique risks of immutable biometric data).

behavior, and power. When individuals know they are being observed, their actions may change. When systems predict behavior, decisions may be influenced before they are even made.

The legal challenge is not only to regulate individual tools, but to address the cumulative effect of systems that monitor and shape behavior at scale.

GENERATIVE AI AND THE EXPANSION OF PRIVACY RISK

Generative AI introduces a new layer of complexity. These systems do not simply analyze data. They learn from it and produce outputs that may reflect patterns within that data.[7]

This raises questions about whether personal information embedded in training datasets can be reproduced, inferred, or exposed through outputs. It also raises broader questions about whether publicly available data can be freely used for training without regard to individual expectations of privacy.

Legal frameworks are still evolving in response to these issues. However, the direction is clear. Systems that generate content will be subject to increasing scrutiny regarding the data they are trained on and the outputs they produce.

A LAWYER'S FRAMEWORK FOR AI PRIVACY RISK

One of the most practical contributions at the intersection of AI and law is the ability to ask the right questions.

---

7. OpenAI, *GPT-4 Technical Report* (2023).

Questions That Define Privacy Compliance:

- What is the source of the data?
- Does the dataset contain personal or sensitive information?
- Was informed consent obtained and is it still valid?
- Is the data being used beyond its original purpose?
- Can individuals access, correct, or delete their data?
- What safeguards exist to prevent misuse or leakage?

This framework reflects a broader principle drawn from practice. Responsible AI development is not achieved through assumptions. It is achieved through interrogation.

Lawyer's Note:
The quality of legal oversight depends on the quality of the questions asked.

Artificial intelligence has not rendered privacy law obsolete. It has made it indispensable. As systems become more powerful, the need for clear boundaries becomes more urgent. Data will continue to drive innovation, but it must do so within a framework that respects individual rights and maintains public trust.

The future of artificial intelligence will not be determined solely by technical capability. It will be shaped by whether the systems we build are aligned with the legal and ethical principles that govern their use.

6

AI AND INTELLECTUAL PROPERTY

Who Owns AI-Generated Content and Why It Matters

Artificial intelligence is forcing intellectual property law into unfamiliar territory. At its core, intellectual property is built on a simple premise. Human beings create, and the law protects what they create. Artificial intelligence unsettles this premise by introducing systems that learn from existing works and generate new ones. The question is no longer only who created a work. It is also what it means to create.

At the center of this transformation lies data. Every generative system is trained on vast corpora of text, images, code, and other materials. Much of this material is protected by copyright. This raises a foundational legal issue. When a system learns from copyrighted works, is it engaging in lawful transformation, or is it engaging in unauthorized copying. This is not a peripheral debate. It is one of the most consequential legal questions in artificial intelligence.

A STRUCTURAL MODEL: CREATION IN THE AGE OF AI

To understand the intellectual property challenge, it is helpful to think in layers.

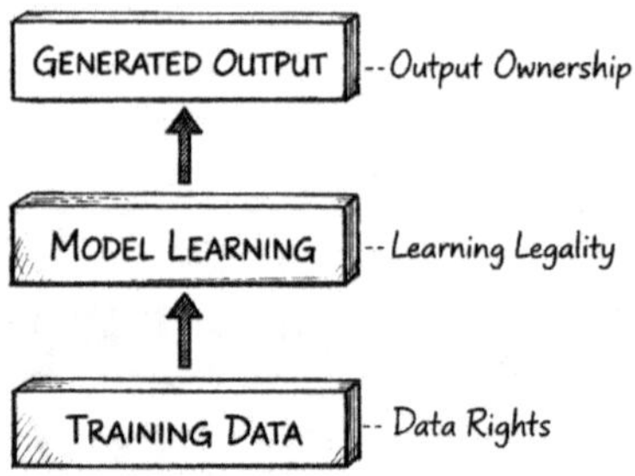

Figure 6.1: The AI Creation Stack

This structure reveals an important truth. Intellectual property issues do not arise only at the output stage. They begin at the data layer and travel through the system.

> **Core Principle:**
> In artificial intelligence, ownership questions begin before creation.

TRAINING DATA AND COPYRIGHT: THE CORE CONFLICT

The use of copyrighted material in training AI systems has become the focal point of litigation.[1] Developers argue that training is transformative.[2] The system does not store or reproduce works in a traditional sense, but instead learns patterns, relationships, and structures.

Rights holders argue the opposite. They contend that entire works are copied into training datasets and used without permission or compensation. In their view, this is not transformation. It is large-scale appropriation.

Courts are now being asked to decide between these competing interpretations. In *Andersen v. Stability AI*, artists alleged that billions of copyrighted images were used to train image-generation systems without authorization.[3] The court allowed key copyright claims to proceed, signaling that training practices may fall within the scope of infringement analysis .

---

1. *Authors Guild v. Google, Inc.*, 804 F.3d 202 (2d Cir. 2015).

2. *Campbell v. Acuff-Rose Music, Inc.*, 510 U.S. 569 (1994).

3. *Andersen v. Stability AI Ltd.*, No. 3:23-cv-00201 (N.D. Cal. 2023).

Similarly, in *Authors Guild v. OpenAI*, authors claim that their books were copied in full to train language models, forming the backbone of commercially valuable systems.[4] The argument is not merely that their works were referenced. It is that they were absorbed into the system itself.

In *Getty Images v. Stability AI*, the scale of alleged copying is central.[5] The complaint asserts that millions of images, along with their metadata, were used without authorization to train models that can now generate competing content.

These cases reflect a broader legal uncertainty. Existing copyright law was not designed for systems that learn from entire corpora of human expression.

Framing Question:
Is learning from a work the same as copying it?

THE FAIR USE QUESTION

At the center of these disputes lies the doctrine of fair use. Courts must determine whether training AI systems constitutes a permissible transformative use or an infringement of exclusive rights. This analysis will likely turn on several factors. Whether the use is transformative. Whether it affects the market for the original work. Whether the amount of the work used is reasonable. And whether the purpose is commercial.

Artificial intelligence complicates each of these factors. Training requires large-scale ingestion of data, often including entire works. The outputs may compete with the original creators. And the systems themselves are frequently deployed for commercial purposes. The outcome of this debate will shape the future of AI development. If training is considered fair use, innovation may accelerate. If it is not, the cost of building AI systems may increase significantly.

---

4. *Authors Guild v. OpenAI Inc.*, No. 1:23-cv-08292 (S.D.N.Y. filed Sept. 19, 2023)

5. *Getty Images (US), Inc. v. Stability AI, Ltd.*, No. 3:25-cv-06891 (N.D. Cal. filed Aug. 14, 2025); *Getty Images (US) Inc. v. Stability AI Ltd.* [2025] EWHC 2863 (Ch)

AI-GENERATED WORKS AND THE LIMITS OF AUTHORSHIP

Even if the training process is resolved, another question emerges at the output stage. Who owns what the system produces. Current U.S. law maintains a clear position. Copyright protects works created by human authors. Where a work is generated entirely by an AI system without meaningful human input, it is not eligible for copyright protection. [6]

This principle was reaffirmed when the U.S. Copyright Office rejected applications for AI-generated works lacking human authorship. Courts have similarly emphasized that authorship requires human creativity.[7] This creates a practical implication for creators. Using AI as a tool does not eliminate authorship. However, relying entirely on AI without meaningful human involvement may result in a loss of protection.

> **Core Principle:**
> Control over the process determines control over the rights.

THE INVENTOR PROBLEM IN PATENT LAW

Patent law faces a parallel challenge. It requires that inventions be attributed to human inventors. This requirement has been tested in cases involving AI-generated inventions. In the DABUS litigation, attempts were made to list an AI system as the inventor of a patent. Courts across multiple jurisdictions rejected this approach, holding that inventors must be natural persons.[8]

This reflects a deeper policy concern. Intellectual property law is not only about recognizing outputs. It is about assigning responsibility and incentive. If machines are recognized as inventors, the foundation of the system begins to shift.

---

6. U.S. Copyright Office, *Copyright Registration Guidance: Works Containing Material Generated by Artificial Intelligence* (2023).

7. *Thaler v. Perlmutter*, 687 F. Supp. 3d 140 (D.D.C. 2023), *aff'd*, No. 23-5233 (D.C. Cir. Mar. 18, 2025), *cert. denied*, No. 25-449 (U.S. Mar. 2, 2026)

8. *Thaler v. Vidal*, 43 F.4th 1207 (Fed. Cir. 2022), *cert. denied*, 143 S. Ct. 1783 (2023).

At the same time, AI is increasingly involved in the inventive process. Systems can generate ideas, optimize designs, and identify solutions. The line between assistance and authorship is becoming more difficult to define.

TRADE SECRETS AND THE PROBLEM OF DISCLOSURE

While copyright and patent law focus on disclosure and protection, trade secret law operates differently.[9] It protects information that derives value from not being publicly known. Many AI systems rely on trade secret protection for their models, datasets, and processes. This creates tension with demands for transparency.

Regulators, courts, and users increasingly call for insight into how systems are trained and how decisions are made. Companies, however, may resist such disclosure, arguing that it would expose proprietary information. Legal disputes have already begun to reflect this tension. In cases involving alleged misappropriation of AI systems and datasets, courts are being asked to determine whether access to such systems constitutes lawful use or theft. The issue is not merely technical. It is structural.

> **Framing Concept:**
> The more valuable the system, the stronger the incentive to keep it secret. The more powerful the system, the stronger the demand to make it transparent.

A PRACTICAL FRAMEWORK: QUESTIONS THAT DEFINE IP RISK IN AI

One of the most useful ways to approach intellectual property in AI is through structured inquiry.

9. Uniform Trade Secrets Act (UTSA); Defend Trade Secrets Act of 2016, 18 U.S.C. § 1836.

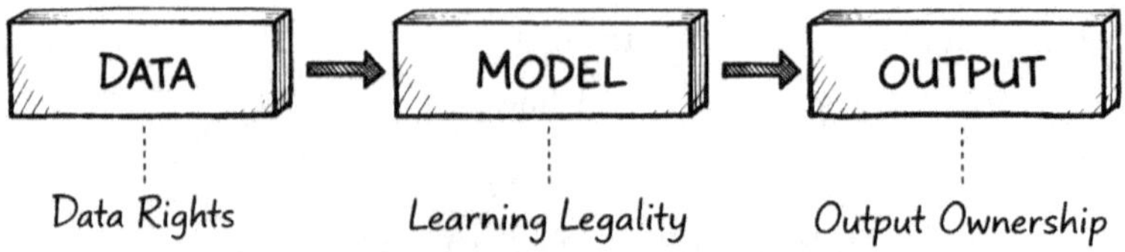

Figure 6.2: The Intellectual Property Risk Framework

The Intellectual Property Risk Framework

Data:

- What is the source of the data?
- Is it copyrighted or proprietary?
- Was authorization obtained?

Model:

- Does the system store or reproduce elements of the data?
- Is the training process legally defensible?

Output:

- Does the output resemble protected works?
- Is there meaningful human contribution?
- Who owns the result?

This framework reflects a central insight from practice. Intellectual property compliance is not achieved by focusing on one stage. It requires examining the entire system.

Lawyer's Note:
Every AI system should be audited from input to output.

THE BROADER TRANSFORMATION

Artificial intelligence is not simply testing intellectual property law. It is reshaping it. Copyright law must now address learning systems. Patent law must account for machine-assisted invention. Trade secret law must balance secrecy with accountability. These are not isolated adjustments. They represent a shift in how law understands creation, ownership, and control.

As a final reflection on this, Artificial intelligence does not eliminate the need for intellectual property law. It expands it. As systems become more capable, the question is no longer whether the law applies. It is how it applies in a context where creation is distributed, learning is continuous, and outputs are generated at scale. The future of intellectual property will depend on how effectively legal systems adapt to this new reality.

7

AI AND LIABILITY

Who Is Responsible When AI Causes Harm

Artificial Intelligence introduces a fundamental challenge to legal systems: harm without clear authorship. When a self-driving vehicle causes an accident, when an algorithm denies someone access to housing or credit, or when an AI system produces dangerously inaccurate medical advice, the consequences are immediate and real. Yet unlike traditional tools, AI systems do not simply execute instructions written by a human. They learn from data, adapt over time, and generate outcomes through processes that are not always fully predictable or explainable.

Legal systems, however, are not designed to accommodate ambiguity in responsibility. At the core of law is a simple expectation: harm must be traceable to a responsible party. Victims must be compensated, and actors must be held accountable. Artificial intelligence complicates this expectation by distributing decision-making across multiple layers and actors. The result is not the disappearance of responsibility, but its transformation. Responsibility becomes diffuse, layered, and contested, requiring new ways of thinking about liability in an automated world.

THE RESPONSIBILITY GAP

To understand liability in artificial intelligence, it is necessary to examine how AI systems alter the structure of causation. In traditional systems, responsibility is relatively straightforward. A human actor uses a tool to make a decision, and any resulting harm can typically be traced back to that individual or the manufacturer of the tool. The chain of causation is linear and identifiable.

AI systems disrupt this clarity. Decisions are no longer made directly by humans, but by models trained on large datasets and shaped by complex statistical processes. These models operate within systems that involve multiple contributors, including developers, data providers, deploying organizations, and end users.

This creates what can be described as a responsibility gap.[1] Harm occurs, but identifying a single responsible actor becomes difficult because:

- Decision-making is mediated by the model;
- The model's behavior is shaped by data from diverse and sometimes opaque sources;
- Systems may evolve after deployment; and
- Outcomes may not be fully foreseeable at the point of design.

Despite this complexity, the law does not accept the absence of responsibility. Instead, it seeks to redistribute responsibility across the system.

1. Andreas Matthias, *The Responsibility Gap: Ascribing Responsibility for the Actions of Learning Automata*, 6 Ethics & Info. Tech. 175 (2004).

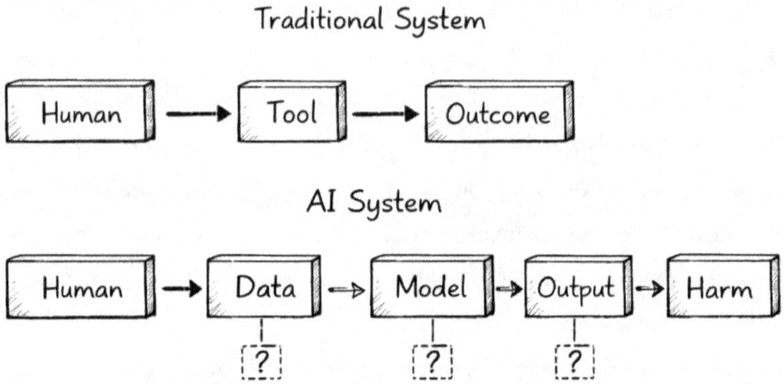

Figure 7.1: The Responsibility Gap

In traditional systems, responsibility is directly traceable. In Al systems, responsibility is distributed across multiple layers, making attribution more complex.

PRODUCT LIABILITY: IS AI A PRODUCT?

One of the most direct approaches to AI liability is to treat AI systems as products. Product liability law imposes strict responsibility on manufacturers when defective products cause harm.[2] This form of liability does not require proof of negligence. Instead, it focuses on whether the product was defective in design, manufacture, or warning. Applying this framework to AI systems raises important questions. If an AI system is treated as a product, then developers may be considered manufacturers, the model itself may be considered the product, and harmful outputs may be viewed as evidence of a defect.

Consider the case of an autonomous vehicle that fails to recognize a pedestrian due to flaws in its training data or model design. If the system is classified as a product, liability may arise even if the developers exercised reasonable care. The focus would shift to whether the system was safe for its intended use. The challenge lies in classification. Courts have not reached a consistent position on whether software, particularly adaptive AI systems, should be treated as products or services.[3] This distinction is critical. If AI is treated as a service, strict liability may not apply, and plaintiffs would instead need to prove negligence.

---

2. Restatement (Third) of Torts: Products Liability § 1 (1998).

3. *Anderson v. TikTok Tech. Ltd.*, 115 F.4th 232 (3d Cir. 2024).

NEGLIGENCE AND THE EXPANDING DUTY OF CARE

Where product liability is uncertain or unavailable, negligence becomes the primary framework for evaluating responsibility. Negligence requires a showing that a party failed to exercise reasonable care under the circumstances.[4] In the context of AI, this duty extends across the entire lifecycle of a system, from development to deployment and ongoing operation.

Developers and organizations deploying AI systems are expected to anticipate foreseeable risks and take steps to mitigate them. This includes ensuring that training data is appropriate, testing models rigorously before deployment, monitoring system performance in real-world environments, and updating systems when risks or defects become apparent.

Failure at any of these stages may constitute a breach of duty. For example, deploying an AI system without adequate testing in complex or high-risk environments may expose an organization to liability if harm occurs. Similarly, failing to address known flaws in a system after deployment may be viewed as negligent conduct. The central question in negligence cases involving AI is not simply whether harm occurred, but whether the harm was reasonably foreseeable and preventable.[5]

PROFESSIONAL RESPONSIBILITY IN AN AI-ASSISTED WORLD

AI systems are increasingly integrated into professional practice. Lawyers, doctors, financial advisors, and other professionals now rely on AI tools to assist with decision-making. This integration does not reduce professional responsibility. In many cases, it heightens it. Professionals are expected to exercise independent judgment, even when assisted by AI. The use of AI does not transfer responsibility to the system. Instead, it introduces an additional layer of risk that must be managed carefully.

---

4. Restatement (Second) of Torts § 282 (1965).

5. *Palsgraf v. Long Island R.R. Co.*, 248 N.Y. 339 (1928).

In legal practice, reliance on AI-generated content without verification can lead to sanctions and malpractice claims. Courts have made clear that while AI tools may assist in drafting or research, attorneys remain fully responsible for the accuracy of their submissions.[6] In medicine, diagnostic tools powered by AI can provide recommendations, but physicians must critically evaluate those recommendations. Blind reliance on AI outputs may constitute a breach of the standard of care.

Across professions, a consistent principle emerges: AI can assist decision-making, but it cannot replace accountability.

Callout (Professional Warning):

Reliance on artificial intelligence does not reduce professional responsibility. It increases the duty to verify.

REAL-WORLD ILLUSTRATIONS OF AI LIABILITY

The challenges of AI liability are already visible in real-world cases. In autonomous vehicle incidents, accidents involving self-driving systems have raised complex questions about responsibility. Liability may involve the vehicle manufacturer, the software developer, the safety driver, or a combination of these actors. Determining fault requires careful analysis of system design, user behavior, and environmental conditions.

In other contexts, automated decision-making systems have produced harmful outcomes when deployed without adequate safeguards. Algorithmic systems used in public administration and private industry have, in some cases, denied individuals benefits or opportunities based on flawed models. These systems can amplify errors at scale, affecting large numbers of people simultaneously.

In healthcare, AI systems designed to assist with diagnosis or treatment have occasionally produced unsafe or misleading outputs. These cases highlight the importance of human oversight and the risks associated with over-reliance on automated systems. Across these examples, harm is rarely the result of a single failure. It typically arises from a combination of design decisions, data limitations, and human actions.

---

6. *Mata v. Avianca, Inc.*, 678 F. Supp. 3d 443 (S.D.N.Y. 2023).

THE CAUSATION CHALLENGE

One of the most difficult aspects of AI liability is establishing causation. Traditional legal analysis depends on identifying a clear link between an action and a harm. AI systems complicate this process in several ways. Many systems operate as "black boxes," meaning their internal reasoning is not easily interpretable.[7] This makes it difficult to explain why a particular outcome occurred.

In addition, AI systems often involve multiple actors. Data may come from one source, the model may be developed by another, and the system may be deployed by a third party. Each actor contributes to the outcome, but none may be solely responsible. Furthermore, AI systems may change over time. Models that learn continuously may behave differently after deployment, raising questions about when and where a defect arose. These factors make it more difficult to prove causation and assign liability using traditional methods.

EMERGING APPROACHES TO AI LIABILITY

Recognizing these challenges, legal systems are beginning to explore new approaches to assigning responsibility. One approach is to impose stricter liability on high-risk AI systems.[8] Under this model, organizations deploying systems in areas such as healthcare, transportation, or finance may be held liable regardless of fault. This reflects the principle that those who benefit from high-risk technologies should also bear the associated risks.

At the same time, such approaches raise important concerns. Overly rigid liability frameworks may discourage innovation, particularly where organizations face uncertainty about how responsibility will be assessed. If the legal risks associated with deploying AI systems become too high or unpredictable, firms may delay or avoid adopting technologies that could otherwise deliver significant societal benefits.

A balanced approach is therefore necessary. Legal frameworks must protect individuals from harm while allowing space for responsible innovation. When properly developed and governed, AI systems can improve decision-making, increase efficiency, and expand

---

7. Frank Pasquale, *The Black Box Society* (2015).

8. European Union Artificial Intelligence Act (EU AI Act), Regulation (EU) 2024/1689.

access to services. The goal is not to restrict AI, but to ensure that its deployment is both beneficial and accountable.

Another approach involves mandatory insurance schemes. Organizations deploying AI systems may be required to carry insurance to ensure that affected individuals are compensated, even where liability is difficult to establish. This shifts the focus from fault to compensation.

A third approach is the development of shared liability frameworks, under which responsibility is distributed across developers, deployers, and users based on their respective roles in the system.[9]

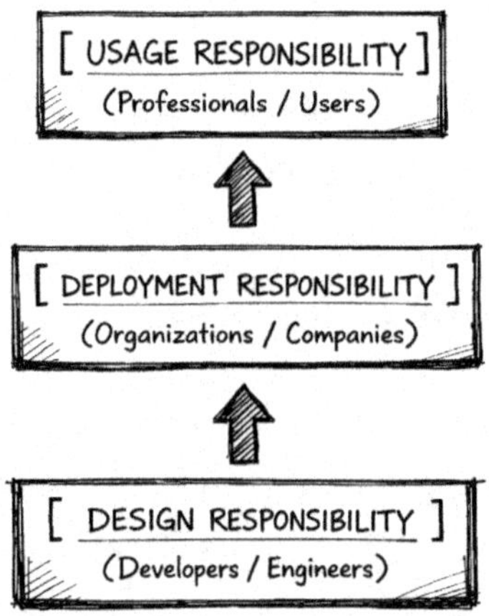

Figure 7.2: The AI Liability Stack

DISTRIBUTED RESPONSIBILITY

AI systems are rarely the product of a single actor. They are created, trained, deployed, and used by different parties, each of whom contributes to the system's behavior.

This creates a model of distributed responsibility, in which liability may be shared across multiple actors. Developers may be responsible for design flaws, data providers for biased or inaccurate data, deploying organizations for misuse or lack of oversight, and users for improper reliance on system outputs.

9. Andrew D. Selbst et al., *Fairness and Abstraction in Sociotechnical Systems*, 134 Harv. L. Rev. 1223 (2019).

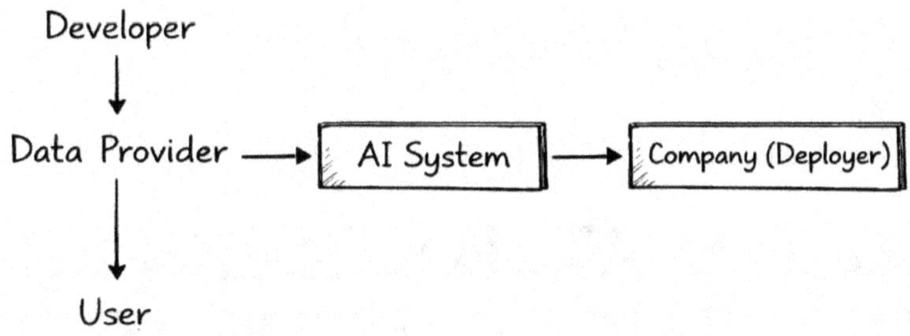

Figure 7.3: Distributed Liability Model

ACCOUNTABILITY IN AN AUTOMATED WORLD

Artificial Intelligence does not eliminate responsibility. It redistributes it. The central challenge for law is not whether AI systems can act autonomously, but how to ensure that accountability remains clear in systems where decision-making is distributed, complex, and evolving.

As AI systems become more powerful and more deeply integrated into society, the need for clear and effective liability frameworks will only increase. Without such frameworks, trust in these systems will erode. With them, innovation can proceed alongside accountability.

At its core, one legal principle remains constant:
Ubi Jus Ibi Remeduim – Where there is wrong, there is a remedy.

8

AI-GENERATED EVIDENCE AND THE CRISIS OF AUTHENTICITY

When Seeing Is No Longer Believing

For much of modern legal history, courts have operated on a quiet but powerful assumption: that audiovisual evidence reflects reality.[1] Photographs, video recordings, and audio files were treated as neutral witnesses, capturing events as they occurred. The law did not require perfection. It required only a reasonable basis to believe that what was presented was what it claimed to be. That assumption is no longer stable.

Artificial intelligence has introduced a fundamental rupture in the relationship between evidence and truth. Today, it is possible to generate highly convincing images, videos, and audio recordings that depict events that never occurred. These outputs do not distort reality. They replace it. The legal system is therefore confronting a new and unsettling question: not whether evidence is persuasive, but whether it is real.

THE TRADITIONAL MODEL OF EVIDENCE

Authentication rules were deliberately designed to be practical. Courts set a relatively low threshold for admissibility because disputes about authenticity were expected to

1. Federal Rules of Evidence 901; Edward J. Imwinkelried, *Evidentiary Foundations* (10th ed. 2018).

be resolved through cross-examination and evaluation by the factfinder.[2] The judge's role was limited to ensuring that there was enough evidence for a reasonable person to conclude that the item was what it purported to be.

This approach worked because digital evidence carried identifiable signals of origin. A photograph reflected light captured at a moment in time. A recording preserved a sequence of real events. Even when manipulation occurred, it was usually detectable through inconsistencies in structure, metadata, or human testimony. These assumptions formed the basis of what is often described as the silent witness doctrine.[3]

The Silent Witness Assumption

Digital evidence was historically trusted because it was understood to:

- Capture reality rather than create it
- Preserve events rather than simulate them
- Reflect a real-world source

Artificial intelligence challenges each of these assumptions.

FROM RECORDING REALITY TO GENERATING IT

Generative AI does not operate as a recording tool. It operates as a construction system. Instead of capturing events, it produces outputs based on patterns learned from vast datasets. The distinction is subtle but profound.

A traditional recording depends on a real-world event. A synthetic output depends only on statistical probability. It can produce a face that has never existed, a voice that was never spoken, or a scene that never occurred. Yet the result may appear indistinguishable from reality. This shift marks a transition from evidence as documentation to evidence as simulation.

2. Federal Rules of Evidence 901(a).

3. *United States v. Taylor*, 530 F.2d 639 (5th Cir. 1976).

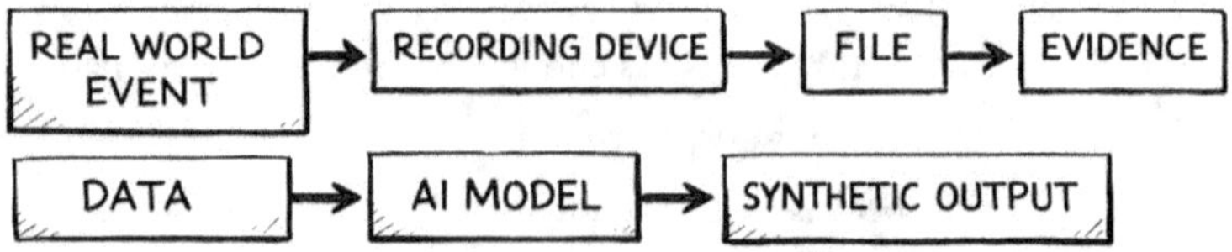

Figure 8.1: From Capture to Generation

THE AUTHENTICATION GAP

At the center of this transformation is a widening gap between how evidence appears and what it actually represents. Traditional authentication relies on cues such as appearance, context, metadata, and human recognition.[4] These cues were once sufficient because falsification was limited and detectable. AI systems, however, are capable of replicating each of these signals with remarkable precision.

A video can now appear consistent, contain plausible metadata, and be confidently identified by a witness, while being entirely fabricated. The law's reliance on surface-level indicators of authenticity is therefore increasingly unreliable. This is what can be described as the authentication gap.

The Authentication Gap

The authentication gap emerges when evidence:

- Appears authentic
- Satisfies traditional indicators
- But is artificially generated

In this environment, appearance no longer guarantees truth.

4. Federal Rules of Evidence 901(b)(1), (4).

STRUCTURAL WEAKNESSES IN EXISTING LEGAL FRAMEWORKS

Using the United States as an anchor point, the challenge becomes clearer. Under Rule 901 of the Federal Rules of Evidence, authentication requires only a showing that the evidence is what it claims to be.[5] This standard was intentionally flexible, reflecting the belief that authenticity disputes should generally be resolved by the jury. That belief is now under pressure.

Testimony from a witness with knowledge has long been sufficient to authenticate evidence.[6] Yet AI-generated media can now replicate voices, facial expressions, and mannerisms with such precision that even close acquaintances may be misled. What was once a strength of the system has become a vulnerability.

Similarly, reliance on metadata and internal characteristics is increasingly problematic.[7] AI systems can generate or manipulate file attributes to mimic legitimate recordings, undermining one of the key circumstantial tools used in authentication.

Perhaps the most significant challenge lies in the nature of AI systems themselves. Unlike traditional tools, many AI models function as opaque systems. Their outputs cannot always be traced through a clear, interpretable process. Demonstrating that such a system produces an accurate result is far more complex than verifying the operation of a conventional device.

5. Fed. R. Evid. 901.

6. Fed. R. Evid. 901(b)(1).

7. Fed. R. Evid. 901(b)(4).

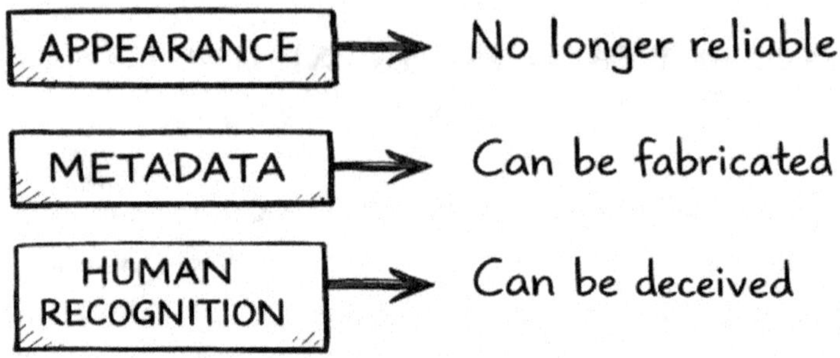

Figure 8.2: The Breakdown of Traditional Signals

THE SYNTHETIC MEDIA PARADOX

One of the most troubling consequences of this shift is the emergence of a paradox at the heart of evidentiary law. Evidence may satisfy procedural requirements for admissibility while being entirely disconnected from reality. A synthetic video can pass through systems designed to verify integrity and still depict an event that never occurred. In other words, the legal system may validate the process through which evidence is introduced without validating the truth of the content itself.

A piece of evidence can be:

- Procedurally valid
- Technically admissible
- Visually convincing

and still be entirely false.

TWO FORMS OF AI EVIDENCE

A useful way to understand the evolving landscape is to distinguish between two categories of AI-related evidence. The first involves situations where the use of AI is acknowledged. In such cases, the central question is not whether the evidence is authentic, but whether the process used to generate or enhance it is reliable. Courts must assess whether the system has introduced distortions, bias, or fabricated elements.

The second involves unacknowledged AI use. Here, synthetic content is presented as if it were a genuine record of events. This creates a direct challenge to authenticity itself and places significant pressure on the court's gatekeeping function. This distinction has become increasingly important in litigation strategy and judicial analysis.

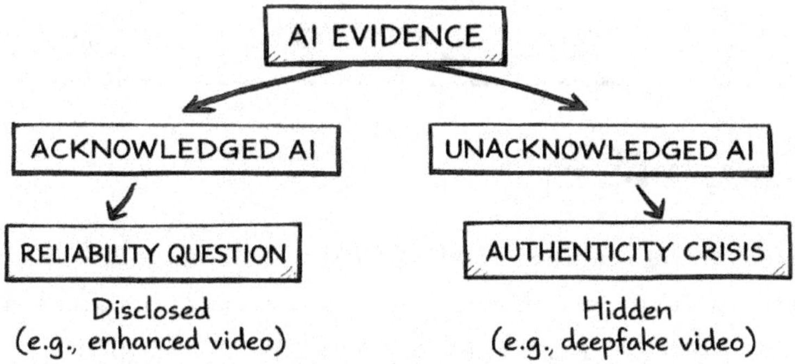

Figure 8.3: Two Paths of AI Evidence

THE EXPANDING ROLE OF THE COURT

The rise of AI-generated evidence is reshaping the role of the judge. Courts are no longer dealing solely with discrete pieces of evidence. They are increasingly required to evaluate the systems that produce those pieces of evidence.[8]

This includes questions such as whether a model is reliable, whether its outputs can be explained, and whether its use introduces risks of distortion or fabrication. The judicial function is therefore expanding from evidentiary gatekeeping to system-level scrutiny.

THE PSYCHOLOGICAL CHALLENGE

Even when synthetic evidence is identified and challenged, its impact may persist. Visual and auditory material carries a level of persuasive force that is difficult to neutralize. Once a juror has seen a compelling image or heard a convincing recording, the impression can remain even after the evidence has been discredited. This creates a structural problem

---

8. Andrew D. Selbst et al., *Fairness and Abstraction in Sociotechnical Systems*, Proc. 2019 Conf. Fairness, Accountability & Transparency 59 (2019)

for the legal system. The harm caused by exposure to false evidence may not be fully reversible.

The Continued Influence Effect:

Discredited evidence can continue to influence judgment. Seeing or hearing something once may be enough to shape belief, even when it is later proven false.

THE LIAR'S DIVIDEND

The proliferation of synthetic media introduces a second and equally serious risk. If anything can be fabricated, then everything can be questioned. This creates an environment in which genuine evidence may be dismissed as artificial. This phenomenon, often referred to as the liar's dividend, allows individuals to evade accountability by exploiting uncertainty.[9] It undermines trust not only in specific pieces of evidence, but in the evidentiary system as a whole.

A GLOBAL SHIFT

Although legal systems differ in structure, the challenge posed by AI-generated evidence is global. Courts in multiple jurisdictions are grappling with similar questions about authenticity, reliability, and fairness.

In the United States, these issues are being addressed through evidentiary doctrine and proposed rule reforms. In the United Kingdom, longstanding assumptions about the reliability of computer-generated evidence are being reconsidered.[10] In the European Union, regulatory frameworks emphasize transparency and human oversight as conditions for trust in automated systems.[11]

---

9. Robert Chesney & Danielle Citron, *Deep Fakes* (2019).

10. *R v. Shepherd* [1993] AC 380 (UKHL).

11. European Union Artificial Intelligence Act (EU AI Act), Regulation (EU) 2024/1689.

Across jurisdictions, a common pattern is emerging. Authentication is no longer treated as a procedural formality. It is becoming a substantive inquiry into how evidence is produced and whether it can be trusted.

FROM TRUST TO VERIFICATION

The legal system is undergoing a transition from passive trust to active verification. Appearance is no longer sufficient. Procedure is no longer enough. Courts must now engage with the underlying systems that produce evidence and evaluate whether those systems can be relied upon. The challenge is not simply to detect deception. It is to rebuild a framework of trust in a world where reality itself can be manufactured.

9

AUTHENTICATING AI EVIDENCE IN COURT

From Low Bar Authentication to Verification Systems

For most of modern legal history, the concept of authentication was never meant to be difficult. Courts did not require absolute proof that evidence was true. They required only a reasonable basis to believe that the evidence was what it purported to be.[1] This approach reflected a practical understanding of litigation. Evidence would be admitted on a relatively low threshold, and its weight would be tested through cross-examination, contradiction, and judicial evaluation.[2]

That model functioned effectively in a world where falsification was limited by technical difficulty. A photograph captured light from a real scene. A recording preserved actual sound. Even where manipulation occurred, it was typically detectable or required sufficient effort that it could be exposed through adversarial testing.

Artificial intelligence has fundamentally altered that landscape. The legal system is no longer dealing with manipulated evidence alone. It is dealing with evidence that can be entirely fabricated while appearing indistinguishable from reality. This development

---

1. Fed. R. Evid. 901(a).

2. John Henry Wigmore, *Evidence in Trials at Common Law* (Chadbourn rev. 1970).

places pressure on a foundational assumption of evidence law. Authentication is no longer simply a gateway question. It has become a central problem of legal reliability.

The challenge is therefore not incremental. It is structural. Courts must now determine whether existing doctrines can withstand a world in which appearance, metadata, and even human recognition can be convincingly simulated.

THE LIMITS OF RULE 901 IN AN AI ENVIRONMENT

At the core of modern authentication doctrine lies Rule 901.[3] The rule requires only that a party produce evidence sufficient to support a finding that the item is what it claims to be. This standard was deliberately designed to be permissive. It reflects the belief that most evidentiary disputes should be resolved by the factfinder rather than excluded at the threshold. That design is now under strain.

Traditional methods of authentication rely on forms of proof that assume a stable relationship between evidence and reality. Testimony from a witness with knowledge has long been considered sufficient to establish authenticity.[4] Distinctive characteristics such as appearance, content, and internal patterns have served as circumstantial indicators of origin.[5] Evidence describing a process or system has been accepted where it demonstrates that the system produces an accurate result.[6] Each of these methods is now vulnerable.

Human recognition can no longer be treated as reliable when AI systems can replicate voices, faces, and mannerisms with near-perfect fidelity. Distinctive characteristics have lost their evidentiary value where metadata and file structures can be artificially generated to mimic legitimate sources. The notion of a reliable system becomes more complex when the system itself is opaque, adaptive, and not fully explainable even to its creators.

The result is a widening gap between doctrinal assumptions and technological reality. The law continues to apply a standard built for a different era, while the nature of evidence has fundamentally changed.

---

3. Fed. R. Evid. 901.

4. Fed. R. Evid. 901(b)(1).

5. Fed. R. Evid. 901(b)(4).

6. Fed. R. Evid. 901(b)(9).

The Authentication Gap:

Authentication assumes that evidence reflects reality. AI allows evidence to simulate reality. The legal test has remained stable, but the underlying truth conditions have shifted.

THE PARADOX OF SELF-AUTHENTICATION

If Rule 901 represents a low threshold, Rule 902 was designed to lower it even further.[7] By allowing certain categories of evidence to be admitted without live testimony, the rule reduces cost and procedural burden. In ordinary cases, this promotes efficiency without undermining fairness.[8] In the context of AI-generated evidence, however, this efficiency creates a deeper problem.

Self-authentication focuses on whether a record has been produced and maintained through a reliable process. It does not examine whether the content of that record corresponds to any real-world event. This distinction becomes critical when dealing with synthetic media. A video may be properly certified as having been generated or stored by a system that functions as expected. That certification does not address whether the video depicts something that actually occurred.

This creates a paradox within evidentiary doctrine. A piece of evidence may satisfy procedural requirements for admissibility while being entirely disconnected from reality. The system confirms integrity of handling, but not authenticity of content.. This paradox exposes a deeper limitation within traditional rules. They were designed to verify origin and preservation, not to interrogate fabrication at scale.

---

7. Fed. R. Evid. 902.

8. Fed. R. Evid. 902(13)–(14).

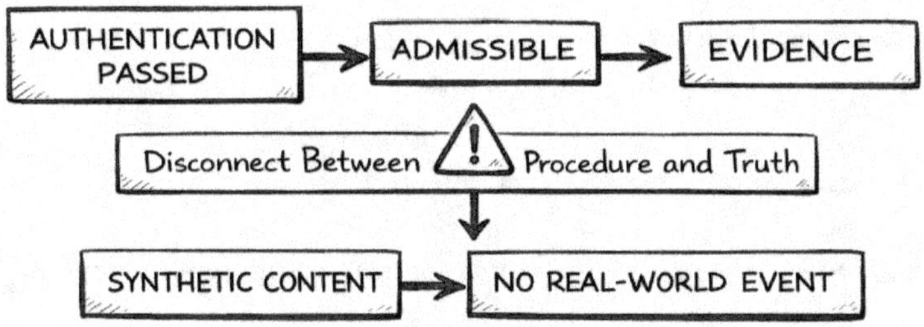

Figure 9.1: The Authentication vs Reality Gap

FROM AUTHENTICATION TO VERIFICATION

The emerging challenge requires a conceptual shift in how courts understand evidence. Authentication is concerned with identity. It asks whether a piece of evidence is what it claims to be. Verification, by contrast, is concerned with origin and process.[9] It asks how the evidence came into existence and whether that process can be trusted.

In an AI-driven environment, identity is easily constructed. A fabricated video can convincingly present itself as a recording of an event. Verification, however, requires a deeper inquiry into provenance, including the history of the file, the systems used to generate or process it, and the conditions under which it was created.

This shift is already visible in evolving legal discourse. Courts are increasingly required to look beyond surface indicators and engage with the systems that produce evidence.[10] The focus is moving from what the evidence appears to be toward how it was produced and whether that production process can be validated.

---

9. Silverman, C. (Ed.), Verification Handbook: A Definitive Guide to Verifying Digital Content for Emergency Coverage (2014).

10. Andrew D. Selbst et al., Deconstructing Design Decisions: Why Courts Must Interrogate Machine Learning and Other Technologies, 85 Ohio St. L.J. 415 (2024).

The Structural Shift:

- Authentication answers: what is this?
- Verification answers: how was this created?

In an AI world, the second question becomes more important than the first.

BURDEN SHIFTING AND THE EMERGENCE OF RULE 901(c)

One of the most significant responses to these challenges is the proposal to modify the structure of authentication itself. The proposed Rule 901(c) introduces a burden-shifting mechanism that reflects the realities of synthetic media.[11] Under this approach, the party challenging the evidence must first make a credible showing that the evidence could be AI-generated or manipulated.[12] This threshold is designed to prevent speculative or frivolous objections from disrupting proceedings. Once that showing is made, however, the evidentiary burden shifts.

The proponent of the evidence must then demonstrate that the evidence is more likely than not authentic.[13] This represents a significant departure from traditional doctrine, where the burden on the proponent is relatively light and disputes are typically resolved by the jury. The rationale for this shift is grounded in practical considerations. The party offering the evidence is usually in the best position to explain its provenance, including how it was created, stored, and transmitted. Requiring that party to provide a more robust foundation reflects the asymmetry of information that characterizes AI-generated evidence.

This proposal also reflects a broader movement toward pretrial judicial gatekeeping. By requiring courts to assess authenticity before evidence reaches the jury, the rule seeks to prevent the irreversible impact of exposure to convincing but false material.

---

11. Proposed evidentiary reform model addressing authentication challenges posed by AI-generated and synthetic media.

12. Fed. R. Evid. 104(a).

13. *Bourjaily v. United States*, 483 U.S. 171 (1987).

Figure 9.2: Burden Shifting in AI Evidence

A PROPOSED DISCLOSURE REQUIREMENT FOR AI-GENERATED EVIDENCE

In addition to burden-shifting frameworks such as proposed Rule 901(c), a complementary reform may be necessary at the threshold stage of admissibility. Legal systems should consider requiring parties who seek to tender computer-generated evidence to disclose whether the evidence was generated, modified, or processed using artificial intelligence systems.

Where AI has been used, the proponent should be required to demonstrate that such involvement does not affect the authenticity or accuracy of the evidence. This preliminary obligation would ensure that courts are not evaluating evidence under incomplete or misleading assumptions about its origin. This shifts the inquiry from whether AI was used to whether its use compromises the integrity of the evidence.

Such a requirement would not eliminate adversarial testing. Rather, it would structure it more effectively. Once the proponent satisfies this initial burden, the opposing party may challenge the evidence under existing or proposed frameworks, including Rule 901(c). The proponent would then have the opportunity to respond, after which the court would determine admissibility.

This approach reflects a more balanced allocation of responsibility. It recognizes that the party offering the evidence is typically in the best position to explain how it was created, while also preserving the opposing party's right to contest its reliability. In an environment where AI-generated content may be indistinguishable from reality, placing the entire burden on the opposing party risks undermining fairness within the evidentiary process. This creates a structured evidentiary sequence in which disclosure precedes challenge, and challenge precedes judicial determination.

While disclosure and burden-shifting address questions of authenticity, a separate challenge arises where AI systems generate outputs that function as analytical conclusions.

RULE 707 AND THE PROBLEM OF MACHINE-GENERATED EXPERTISE

A separate but related issue arises when AI systems produce outputs that function as analytical conclusions rather than mere representations. These outputs may include classifications, predictions, or reconstructions that resemble expert testimony.[14]

In traditional doctrine, such testimony is subject to rigorous scrutiny under standards of reliability. The expert must demonstrate that their methods are grounded in sufficient data, based on reliable principles, and applied appropriately to the facts of the case. AI systems complicate this framework.[15] Their outputs are often presented as neutral or objective, even though they are the result of complex processes involving training data, model architecture, and probabilistic inference. Treating these outputs as simple evidence risks bypassing the safeguards that apply to expert testimony.

The proposed Rule 707 addresses this concern by requiring machine-generated outputs to meet the same reliability standards as human experts.[16] This ensures that courts evaluate not only the output itself, but the methodology and assumptions that produced it. This development reflects a deeper recognition. AI systems are not passive tools. They are active interpreters of data, and their outputs must be treated accordingly.

The Hidden Expert:

AI systems do not merely display information. They generate conclusions based on data and models. This makes them functional experts within the evidentiary process.

---

14. Fed. R. Evid. 702.

15. *Daubert v. Merrell Dow Pharmaceuticals, Inc.*, 509 U.S. 579 (1993).

16. Proposed Rule 707 framework for AI-generated analytical outputs.

TECHNICAL VERIFICATION AND THE RISE OF PROVENANCE

As doctrinal frameworks evolve, courts are increasingly turning to technical methods to address the limitations of traditional authentication. These methods focus on establishing a verifiable history of a digital asset rather than relying solely on its appearance or context.

Provenance systems represent one of the most promising developments in this area. By embedding cryptographic signatures and structured metadata into digital content, these systems create a record of how a file was created and modified over time.[17] Each step in the lifecycle of the file can be documented and verified, providing a more robust foundation for authenticity.

Other approaches, such as watermarking and blockchain-based verification, attempt to address similar concerns from different angles.[18] Watermarking seeks to embed identifiable signals within the content itself, while blockchain records provide an immutable record of a file's existence at a specific point in time.

These technologies are not without limitations. Their effectiveness depends on widespread adoption, and they can be circumvented or absent in many real-world scenarios. Nonetheless, they represent a shift toward a more rigorous understanding of evidence, one that prioritizes traceability and transparency over surface-level plausibility.

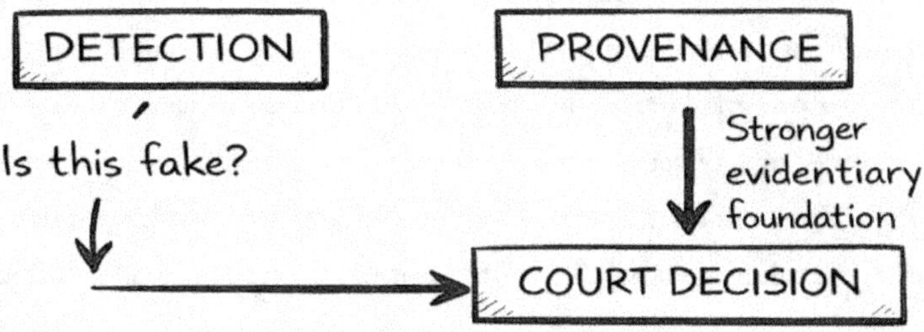

Figure 9.3: Verification vs Detection

17. Coalition for Content Provenance and Authenticity (C2PA), *Technical Specification* (2024).

18. Primavera De Filippi & Aaron Wright, *Blockchain and the Law* (2018).

A GLOBAL LEGAL SHIFT

The challenges posed by AI-generated evidence are not confined to any single jurisdiction. Courts around the world are grappling with similar issues, though their responses reflect different legal traditions and institutional priorities.

In the United States, the emphasis has been on judicial gatekeeping and evidentiary reform, with proposals such as Rule 901(c) and Rule 707 reflecting an effort to adapt existing doctrine. In the United Kingdom, courts are reassessing longstanding assumptions about the reliability of computer-generated evidence, particularly the presumption that systems operate correctly unless proven otherwise.[19] In the European Union, regulatory frameworks emphasize transparency, explainability, and human oversight as essential components of trustworthy AI systems.[20]

Despite these differences, a common trajectory is emerging. Legal systems are moving away from passive reliance on digital evidence and toward active scrutiny of how such evidence is produced.

THE PSYCHOLOGICAL DIMENSION AND THE LIMITS OF LEGAL SOLUTIONS

Even as courts develop more sophisticated frameworks, a fundamental challenge remains. Human cognition is not well-equipped to evaluate synthetic realism. Visual and auditory evidence carries a powerful persuasive effect, and once a juror has been exposed to such material, its influence may persist even if it is later discredited.[21]

At the same time, the existence of AI-generated content introduces a countervailing risk. Parties may exploit the possibility of fabrication to cast doubt on genuine evidence.

---

19. *R v. Shepherd* [1993] AC 380 (UKHL).

20. Regulation (EU) 2024/1689 (Artificial Intelligence Act).

21. Stephan Lewandowsky et al., *Misinformation and Its Correction: Continued Influence and Successful Debiasing*, 13 Psychol. Sci. Pub. Int. 106 (2012).

This phenomenon, often referred to as the liar's dividend, undermines trust in the evidentiary process itself.[22]

The legal system is therefore confronted with a dual challenge. It must guard against the admission of false evidence while also preventing the unjust dismissal of authentic material. Achieving this balance requires not only doctrinal reform, but also a deeper understanding of how evidence is perceived and evaluated.

The Liar's Dividend:

If evidence can be fabricated, it can also be denied. The risk is not only that false evidence will be believed, but that true evidence will be dismissed

TOWARD A SYSTEM OF VERIFIED TRUTH

The transformation of evidence law in the age of artificial intelligence is not merely a matter of updating rules. It requires a rethinking of foundational assumptions about truth, authenticity, and trust.

The traditional model treated authentication as a threshold issue and left questions of reliability to the factfinder. That model is increasingly inadequate in a world where evidence can be convincingly fabricated at scale.

The emerging framework places greater emphasis on verification, provenance, and judicial gatekeeping. It recognizes that the integrity of the legal process depends not only on the admission of evidence, but on the ability to verify the processes that produce it.

The future of evidence law will therefore depend on a fundamental shift. Courts must move beyond asking whether evidence appears authentic. They must develop the tools, standards, and institutional practices necessary to determine whether it can be trusted at all.

22. Robert Chesney & Danielle Citron, *Deep Fakes* (2019).

10

CHALLENGING AI-GENERATED EVIDENCE

How Lawyers Can Prove or Disprove Synthetic Reality

If authentication is the first line of defense against unreliable digital evidence, then challenge is the second, and often more decisive, stage. The emergence of AI-generated and AI-manipulated evidence has fundamentally altered what it means to contest proof in court. Lawyers are no longer dealing solely with documents, recordings, or physical exhibits. They are confronting systems that can generate convincing realities, alter existing records, and obscure the very processes by which evidence is created.

This shift requires a corresponding evolution in legal strategy. Challenging evidence is no longer confined to raising objections or pointing out inconsistencies. It now demands a structured, multi-layered approach that combines procedural tools, technical interrogation, and narrative clarity. The modern advocate must understand not only what the evidence appears to show, but how it came into existence, how it was handled, and whether its underlying processes can withstand scrutiny.

At the center of this new battlefield is a simple but powerful idea. Every digital file carries a history. The strength or weakness of that history often determines whether the evidence survives challenge or collapses under examination.

THE "STORY OF THE FILE"

The most effective way to challenge AI-generated evidence is to shift the focus away from appearance and toward provenance.[1] Courts have historically relied on visual or testimonial confirmation to assess authenticity, but these methods are increasingly unreliable in the face of synthetic media. A deepfake video or AI-generated audio recording may appear entirely convincing, yet still be fundamentally disconnected from reality.

For this reason, practitioners are increasingly adopting what can be described as the "story of the file" approach. This approach treats every piece of digital evidence as a sequence of events rather than a static object. It asks where the file originated, what device or system created it, who had access to it at each stage, and what transformations it underwent before being presented in court.

When these questions are pursued rigorously, the nature of the dispute changes. The issue is no longer whether the evidence looks real, but whether its lifecycle can be verified. Gaps in custody, unexplained transformations, or missing source material become far more significant than surface-level credibility. In many cases, a file that appears persuasive may fail entirely when its history is examined in detail.

This approach also aligns with broader evidentiary principles. Authentication, chain of custody, and reliability are not isolated doctrines. They are interconnected mechanisms for establishing trust. By reconstructing the story of the file, the lawyer exposes the points at which that trust may have been compromised.

The Core Strategy:

A convincing deepfake survives visual inspection. It often fails when its history is examined. The strongest challenge is procedural, not cosmetic.

1. Hany Farid, Mitigating the Harms of Manipulated Media: Confronting Deepfakes and Digital Deception(2025).

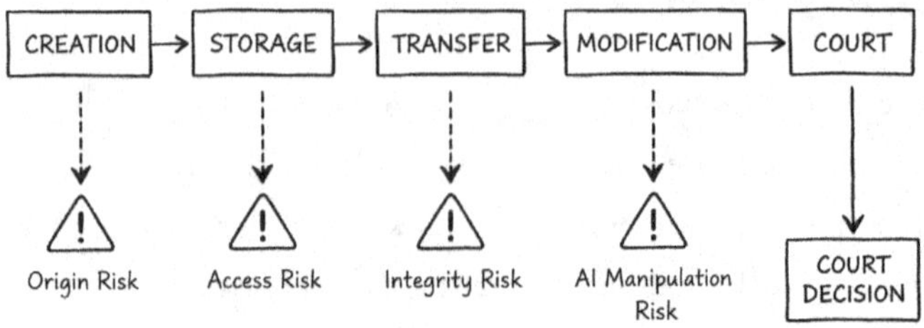

Figure 10.1: The Story of the File

MOTIONS TO SUPPRESS AND STRATEGIC EXCLUSION

One of the most effective ways to challenge AI-generated evidence is to prevent it from reaching the factfinder in the first place. This is typically achieved through pretrial motions that focus on admissibility rather than weight.[2] In criminal cases, this may take the form of a motion to suppress. In both civil and criminal contexts, it often involves arguments grounded in evidentiary balancing and procedural fairness.

AI-generated and AI-enhanced evidence presents unique risks that go beyond traditional concerns. Visual and audio material carries a strong psychological impact, and jurors may assign it disproportionate weight even when its reliability is uncertain.[3] Courts have increasingly recognized that admitting such evidence can create confusion, invite speculation, and shift the focus away from the central issues in dispute.

This creates a powerful basis for exclusion. The argument is not merely that the evidence is flawed, but that its admission would undermine the fairness of the proceeding. Where the reliability of the evidence cannot be clearly demonstrated, or where its underlying process cannot be explained, the risk of misleading the factfinder may outweigh any probative value it offers.[4]

In practice, this strategy requires careful framing. The lawyer must articulate not only the technical weaknesses of the evidence, but also the broader consequences of allowing

2. Fed. R. Evid. 403.

3. Stephan Lewandowsky et al., *Misinformation and Its Correction: Continued Influence and Successful Debiasing*, 13 Psychol. Sci. Pub. Int. 106 (2012).

4. Fed. R. Evid. 403.

it into the courtroom. By emphasizing the potential for confusion and prejudice, the advocate shifts the court's focus from curiosity about the technology to concern about procedural integrity.

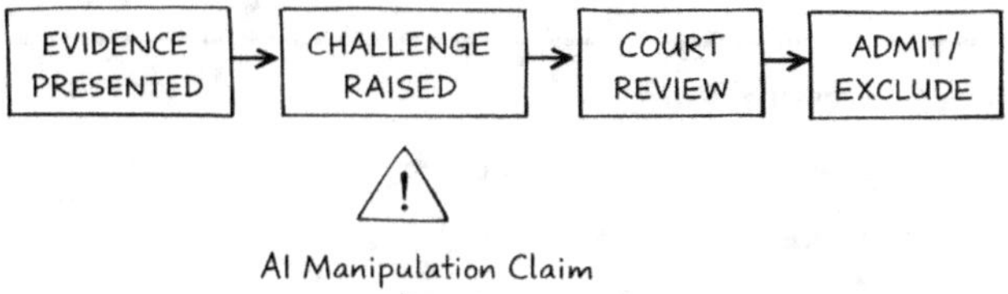

Figure 10.2: Challenging AI Evidence Flow

DAUBERT CHALLENGES AND THE QUESTION OF RELIABILITY

When AI evidence is supported by expert testimony, the battleground shifts from admissibility to methodology. Courts do not simply accept expert conclusions at face value.[5] They require that those conclusions be grounded in reliable principles, supported by sufficient data, and applied in a manner that can be tested and evaluated.[6]

AI systems complicate this analysis in several ways. First, many models operate as "black boxes," producing outputs without transparent reasoning processes. This makes it difficult for experts to explain how a particular conclusion was reached. Second, validation remains inconsistent. A system that performs well under controlled conditions may produce unreliable results when applied to real-world data that differs in quality, format, or context.

Error rates also become critical. Courts expect experts to identify the likelihood of false positives and false negatives, yet many AI tools lack well-established benchmarks.[7] Without this information, it becomes difficult to assess whether a conclusion is trustworthy or merely plausible.

---

5. *Daubert v. Merrell Dow Pharmaceuticals, Inc.*, 509 U.S. 579 (1993).

6. Fed. R. Evid. 702.

7. *Daubert v. Merrell Dow Pharmaceuticals, Inc.*, 509 U.S. 579 (1993).

These limitations provide a strong foundation for challenge. When an expert relies on a system that cannot be fully explained, validated, or tested, the reliability of the evidence itself comes into question. In such cases, the argument is not simply that the evidence is weak, but that it fails to meet the standards required for expert testimony.

The Daubert Pressure Point:

If the system cannot explain itself, and the expert cannot validate it, the evidence should not be admitted.

CROSS-EXAMINATION: EXPOSING TECHNICAL WEAKNESSES

Cross-examination remains one of the most powerful tools for challenging AI-generated evidence, but its effectiveness depends on adapting traditional techniques to modern realities. The goal is not to outmatch the expert on technical detail, but to expose the limits of their conclusions and the assumptions underlying their analysis.

One effective strategy is to highlight the ambiguity of so-called indicators of manipulation. Many features associated with synthetic media, such as visual artifacts, inconsistencies, or distortions, can also arise from benign processes like compression or low-quality recording conditions. By demonstrating that these indicators are not unique to AI-generated content, the lawyer weakens the certainty of the opposing expert's claims.

Another key line of questioning focuses on reproducibility. If the expert's analysis cannot be replicated using the same data and methods, its reliability becomes questionable.[8] This is particularly important where proprietary tools or undisclosed parameters are involved. Without transparency, the conclusions drawn from such tools cannot be independently verified.[9]

Chain of custody also plays a critical role. If the expert relied on a version of the file that has been altered, compressed, or otherwise transformed, the integrity of the analysis may be compromised. By drawing attention to these issues, the advocate shifts the focus from the apparent strength of the evidence to the weaknesses in how it was analyzed.

---

8. *Daubert v. Merrell Dow Pharmaceuticals, Inc.*, 509 U.S. 579 (1993).

9. Danielle Keats Citron, *Technological Due Process*, 85 Wash. U. L. Rev. 1249 (2008).

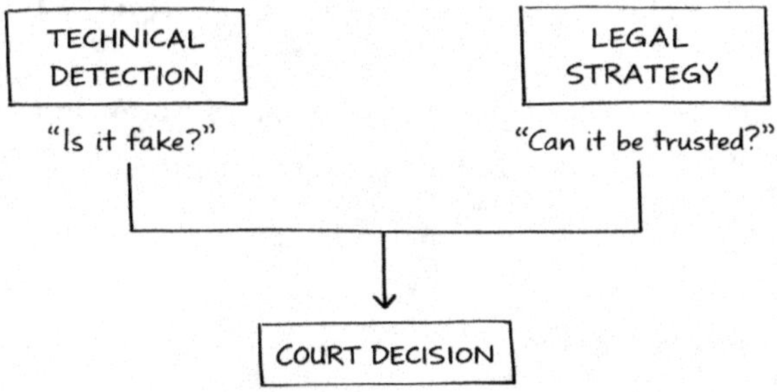

Figure 10.3: Detection vs Legal Doubt

DISCOVERY AND ACCESS TO UNDERLYING EVIDENCE

The ability to challenge AI-generated evidence often depends on access to information that lies beneath the surface. Without access to the original file, the source device, or the processing history, meaningful scrutiny becomes difficult, if not impossible. This makes discovery a central component of any effective challenge strategy.

Lawyers must think beyond the evidence itself and focus on the surrounding data. Metadata, system logs, software versions, and processing records can all provide insight into how a file was created and handled.[10] Where AI tools are involved, this may also include prompts, model versions, and validation documentation.

The failure to preserve or produce this information can have significant consequences. Courts may impose sanctions in civil cases where relevant electronic evidence has been lost, particularly if it cannot be restored or replaced.[11] In criminal proceedings, the failure to preserve potentially useful evidence may raise due process concerns, especially where bad faith is involved.[12]

Ultimately, discovery is not just about obtaining information. It is about testing the completeness and credibility of the opposing party's account. When key pieces of the story are missing, the reliability of the evidence itself is called into question.

---

10. Fed. R. Civ. P. 26(b)(1).

11. Fed. R. Civ. P. 37(e).

12. *Arizona v. Youngblood*, 488 U.S. 51 (1988).

PLATFORM EVIDENCE AND STRUCTURAL LIMITATIONS

In many cases, digital evidence originates from online platforms, introducing additional layers of complexity. Platforms may hold critical information about how content was uploaded, modified, and distributed, but access to that information is often restricted by legal and technical constraints.

This creates a practical challenge for litigants. While platform data can be invaluable in establishing provenance, obtaining it may require navigating regulatory frameworks, issuing subpoenas, and acting within limited retention periods.[13] At the same time, the evidence itself may have undergone multiple transformations through compression, re-encoding, or format changes, each of which can affect its reliability and forensic anal ysis.[14]

These limitations reinforce the importance of early action. The longer a party waits to investigate digital evidence, the greater the risk that critical information will be lost or degraded. In the context of AI-generated evidence, this delay can make the difference between a successful challenge and an unresolved ambiguity.

NARRATIVE STRATEGY AND PERSUASION

Beyond procedural and technical considerations, challenging AI-generated evidence also requires careful attention to narrative. Courts and juries do not evaluate evidence in isolation. They interpret it within a broader story about what happened, who is credible, and what can be trusted.

A lawyer who can clearly explain the risks associated with synthetic media, the limitations of detection methods, and the gaps in the opposing party's account is better positioned to influence how the evidence is perceived. This does not require exaggeration or speculation. In fact, overstating the prevalence of deepfakes can undermine credibility and lead to skepticism about legitimate arguments.

The goal is precision. By focusing on specific weaknesses and clearly articulating why those weaknesses matter, the advocate builds a persuasive case that the evidence should

---

13. Fed. R. Civ. P. 45.

14. Hany Farid, *Digital Forensics in an Era of Synthetic Media* (2022).

not be relied upon. This approach aligns with the broader principles of advocacy, where clarity and credibility often outweigh technical complexity.

Narrative Control:

Do not argue that everything is fake. Show why this evidence cannot be trusted. Precision persuades. Speculation weakens.

THE GLOBAL DIMENSION OF CHALLENGE

The challenge of AI-generated evidence is not confined to any single legal system. Courts across jurisdictions are confronting similar issues, though their approaches differ.[15] In systems that emphasize judicial gatekeeping, the focus is often on pretrial hearings and expert scrutiny. In systems that rely more heavily on presumptions about system reliability, those presumptions are beginning to weaken in light of AI's generative capabilities. Regulatory frameworks in some regions emphasize transparency and explainability as conditions for admissibility and fairness.

Despite these differences, a common pattern is emerging. The burden is shifting toward those who seek to rely on digital evidence to demonstrate not only that it exists, but that it can be trusted.[16]

FROM APPEARANCE TO PROOF

The challenge of AI-generated evidence marks a turning point in legal practice. The traditional assumption that seeing is believing no longer holds. Digital evidence can be fabricated, altered, or enhanced in ways that are difficult to detect and even harder to explain.

In this environment, the role of the lawyer becomes more demanding and more critical. It is no longer enough to question the surface of the evidence. The advocate must interro-

15. Regulation (EU) 2024/1689 (Artificial Intelligence Act); *R v. Shepherd* [1993] AC 380 (UKHL).

16. Fed. R. Evid. 901; Fed. R. Evid. 104(a).

gate its origins, its transformations, and its underlying processes. They must reconstruct the story of the file and expose the points at which that story fails.

This shift does not weaken the legal system. It strengthens it. By demanding greater scrutiny, greater transparency, and greater rigor, courts can adapt to the realities of synthetic media while preserving the integrity of the adjudicative process. The future of advocacy will not depend on who presents the most convincing evidence. It will depend on who can prove that their evidence deserves to be believed.

11

THE FUTURE OF EVIDENCE LAW IN THE AGE OF AI

From Evidence to Systems

For centuries, the law of evidence has operated on a quiet but powerful assumption. Evidence reflects reality. The role of the court is to determine whether that reflection is accurate, reliable, and admissible. That assumption is now under pressure.

Artificial intelligence has introduced a new category of evidentiary risk. Evidence is no longer limited to capturing reality. It can now simulate reality, reconstruct reality, or generate entirely fictional events that are indistinguishable from authentic ones. This shift does not simply create more evidentiary disputes. It alters the nature of what evidence is. As a result, courts are beginning to confront a deeper transformation. They are no longer evaluating isolated pieces of evidence. They are increasingly being asked to evaluate the systems that produce that evidence.

This transition marks a turning point in legal doctrine. The future of evidence law will not be defined solely by rules of admissibility. It will be defined by how legal systems adapt to a world in which reality itself can be manufactured.

FROM EVIDENCE TO SYSTEMS

Traditional evidentiary analysis is object-focused.[1] A photograph, a document, or a recording is examined on its own terms. The inquiry asks whether the item is authentic, relevant, and reliable. This approach assumes that the underlying process that produced the evidence is either simple or inherently trustworthy. AI disrupts that assumption.

Modern evidence is often the output of complex, layered systems involving data inputs, model training, algorithmic processing, and probabilistic inference.[2] In such cases, the reliability of the evidence cannot be assessed by examining the output alone. It depends on the integrity of the entire system that produced it.

This is already reflected in emerging legal discourse. Courts are increasingly recognizing that evaluating AI-generated evidence requires an understanding of how the system operates, including its data sources, design choices, and potential biases.[3] The implication is profound. Evidence law is shifting from a focus on objects to a focus on processes. The question is no longer simply "what is this evidence?" but "what system produced it, and can that system be trusted?"

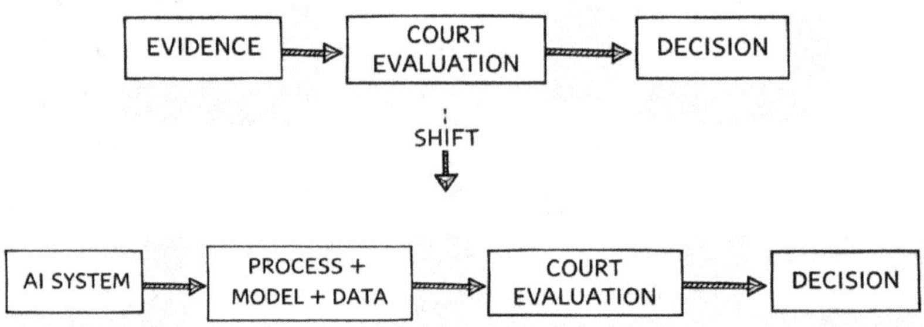

Figure 11.1: From Evidence to Systems

1. Fed. R. Evid. 901.

2. Stuart Russell & Peter Norvig, *Artificial Intelligence: A Modern Approach* (4th ed. 2021).

3. *Daubert v. Merrell Dow Pharmaceuticals, Inc.*, 509 U.S. 579 (1993).

The Structural Shift:

- Old model: evaluate the evidence.
- Transitional model: evaluate whether the system is generally reliable.
- New model: evaluate whether the specific system can be trusted in the context in which it produced the evidence.

Trust moves from the object to the process. While courts have previously considered the reliability of systems that produce evidence, such evaluation was typically limited and peripheral. The system was treated as a supporting mechanism, not the primary subject of inquiry.

Artificial intelligence fundamentally changes that relationship. In AI-driven contexts, the reliability of the evidence cannot be assessed without directly interrogating the system itself. The system is no longer a background consideration. It becomes the central object of evidentiary analysis. This marks a shift from general assumptions of system reliability to case-specific evaluation of system behavior.

EXPLAINABILITY AS A LEGAL REQUIREMENT

One of the most significant consequences of this shift is the growing importance of explainability. Traditional forms of evidence rarely required explanation beyond basic authentication. A witness could testify that a photograph accurately depicted what they saw, and that was often sufficient. AI-generated evidence, however, cannot be evaluated in the same way. Its reliability depends on processes that may be opaque, complex, and difficult to interpret.

This creates a fundamental tension within the legal system. Courts require reasons.[4] They require explanations that can be tested, challenged, and understood. AI systems, particularly advanced machine learning models, do not always provide such explanations.

4. Fed. R. Evid. 702; *Daubert v. Merrell Dow Pharmaceuticals, Inc.*, 509 U.S. 579 (1993).

They produce outputs without revealing the reasoning pathways that led to those outputs.

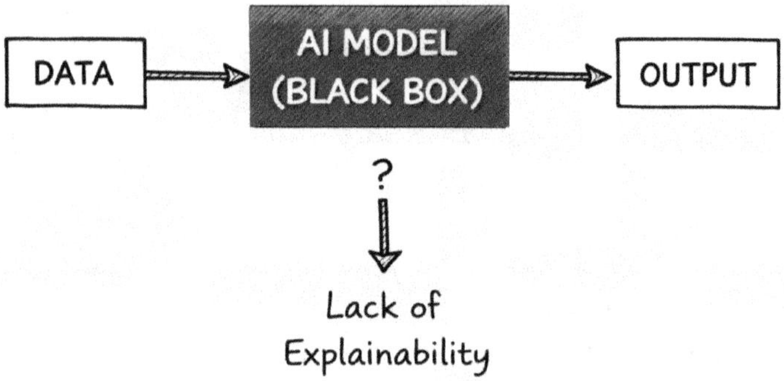

Figure 11.2: The Explainability Problem

As a result, explainability is emerging as a central legal requirement. If an AI system cannot explain how it reached a particular conclusion, its output becomes difficult to evaluate within existing evidentiary frameworks. This does not mean that all opaque systems must be excluded. It means that courts must develop standards for when opacity is acceptable and when it undermines reliability.

This issue is particularly acute in cases involving machine-generated conclusions, such as classification results, predictive scores, or forensic analyses.[5] In these contexts, the absence of explainability is not merely a technical limitation. It is a legal vulnerability.

> **The Explainability Problem:**
>
> Courts do not accept conclusions without reasons. AI often produces conclusions without explanations. This gap must be resolved for evidence to remain reliable.

THE EXPANSION OF JUDICIAL GATEKEEPING

As evidentiary challenges become more complex, the role of the judge is evolving. Historically, judges acted as gatekeepers in a limited sense.[6] They ensured that evidence met

5. Danielle Keats Citron, *Technological Due Process*, 85 Wash. U. L. Rev. 1249 (2008).

6. *Daubert v. Merrell Dow Pharmaceuticals, Inc.*, 509 U.S. 579 (1993).

basic admissibility standards, while leaving most questions of weight and credibility to the jury. This division reflected confidence in the jury's ability to evaluate evidence presented to it. AI-generated evidence complicates this model.

The psychological impact of synthetic media, combined with its potential for deception, creates a risk that juries may be misled even when evidence is later discredited. This has led to an increasing emphasis on pretrial judicial evaluation, where questions of authenticity, reliability, and methodology are addressed before the evidence reaches the factfinder.[7]

This shift is already visible in proposals such as the Proposed Rule 901(c), which introduces a burden-shifting mechanism and requires judges to make more substantive determinations about authenticity at the admissibility stage.[8] It is also reflected in the application of reliability standards to machine-generated outputs, where courts must assess not only whether the evidence exists, but whether the methods used to produce it are trustworthy.[9]

The result is an expansion of judicial responsibility. Judges are no longer simply screening evidence. They are increasingly required to evaluate complex technical systems and to make determinations that were previously left to the adversarial process.

BUILDING A TRUST INFRASTRUCTURE

As the limitations of traditional authentication become more apparent, attention is turning toward the development of a broader trust infrastructure for digital evidence.

This infrastructure includes both legal and technical components. On the legal side, it involves updated rules, clearer standards for admissibility, and procedural mechanisms that allow courts to address AI-related risks effectively. On the technical side, it includes

7. Fed. R. Evid. 104(a).

8. Proposed evidentiary framework addressing AI-related authentication disputes.

9. Fed. R. Evid. 702; *Daubert v. Merrell Dow Pharmaceuticals, Inc.*, 509 U.S. 579 (1993).

tools such as provenance systems, watermarking, and cryptographic verification, which provide additional layers of assurance about the origin and integrity of digital content.[10]

Figure 11.3 — The Trust Infrastructure Model

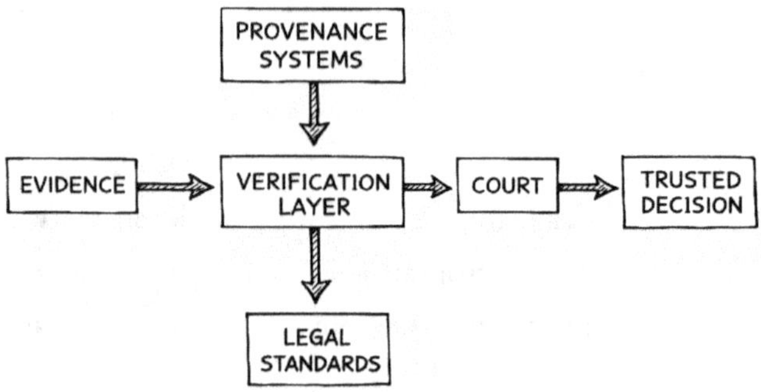

Figure 11.3: The Trust Infrastructure Model

Technologies such as content credentials and cryptographic signatures offer a promising path forward. By embedding verifiable information about how a file was created and modified, these systems allow courts to move beyond surface-level analysis and toward a more robust understanding of evidentiary reliability.

However, these solutions are not universal. Their effectiveness depends on widespread adoption, standardization, and integration into existing workflows. In many cases, evidence will continue to be presented without such safeguards, requiring courts to rely on a combination of technical expertise and legal judgment.

The concept of trust infrastructure therefore extends beyond any single technology. It represents a broader shift toward systems that support transparency, traceability, and accountability in the production of evidence.

Trust Is No Longer Assumed:

In the past, evidence was presumed reliable unless challenged. In the AI era, reliability must be demonstrated. Trust becomes something that is built, not assumed.

10. Coalition for Content Provenance and Authenticity (C2PA), *Technical Specification* (2024).

GLOBAL CONVERGENCE AND DIVERGENCE

The transformation of evidence law is not confined to a single jurisdiction. Courts around the world are grappling with similar challenges, though their responses reflect different legal traditions and regulatory priorities.

In the United States, the emphasis has been on adapting existing evidentiary rules and expanding judicial gatekeeping.[11] In the United Kingdom, longstanding presumptions about the reliability of computer-generated evidence are being reconsidered in light of AI's generative capabilities.[12] In the European Union, regulatory frameworks emphasize transparency, explainability, and human oversight as essential components of trustworthy AI systems.[13]

Despite these differences, a common pattern is emerging. Legal systems are moving toward greater scrutiny of the processes that produce evidence and greater emphasis on the conditions under which that evidence can be trusted. This convergence suggests that the challenges posed by AI are not merely technical or local. They are structural and global, requiring coordinated responses across jurisdictions.

THE RISK OF OVERCORRECTION

While increased scrutiny is necessary, it also carries risks. One potential danger is overcorrection. If courts become excessively skeptical of digital evidence, they may undermine the very function of the legal system. Evidence that is reliable may be excluded or discounted simply because it could have been fabricated. This creates a form of evidentiary paralysis, where uncertainty replaces evaluation.

At the same time, the possibility of AI fabrication creates opportunities for strategic misuse. Parties may invoke the possibility of deepfakes to cast doubt on legitimate evidence, even where there is no credible basis for doing so. This phenomenon, often referred to as the liar's dividend, can erode trust in the adjudicative process.

---

11. Fed. R. Evid. 901; *Daubert v. Merrell Dow Pharmaceuticals, Inc.*, 509 U.S. 579 (1993).

12. *R v. Shepherd* [1993] AC 380 (UKHL).

13. Regulation (EU) 2024/1689 (Artificial Intelligence Act).

The challenge for courts is therefore not simply to increase scrutiny, but to calibrate it. The goal is to develop standards that are rigorous enough to detect and exclude unreliable evidence, while flexible enough to admit evidence that can be reasonably trusted.

The Balance Problem:

Too little scrutiny allows synthetic evidence to deceive. Too much scrutiny allows real evidence to be dismissed. The future of evidence law lies in finding the balance.

INSTITUTIONALIZING TRUST

The future of evidence law will not be defined by any single rule, doctrine, or technology. It will be defined by how legal systems respond to a fundamental shift in the nature of evidence itself. Artificial intelligence has blurred the line between reality and representation. In doing so, it has exposed the limitations of frameworks built on assumptions that no longer hold. The task ahead is not to abandon those frameworks, but to adapt them.

This adaptation requires a move toward verification, explainability, and systemic evaluation. It requires courts to engage with the processes that produce evidence, rather than relying solely on the evidence itself. It requires the development of trust infrastructure that supports transparency and accountability. Most importantly, it requires a recognition that trust is no longer inherent in evidence. It must be established, demonstrated, and maintained.

The future of evidence law will depend not on whether courts can detect deception, but on whether they can build systems that make trust possible in a world where reality can be manufactured.

12

REGULATING AI IN A FRAGMENTED WORLD

Why Global AI Rules Conflict and What That Means for You

Artificial Intelligence does not respect borders. A system designed in California may be trained on data from Europe, deployed through servers in Asia, and used by individuals across Africa. Yet the law remains fundamentally territorial. This tension lies at the heart of modern AI governance.

Unlike earlier technologies, AI is not simply a tool that can be confined within a jurisdiction. It is an ecosystem made up of data, models, infrastructure, and users, all operating across multiple legal systems. As a result, there is no single global framework governing AI. Instead, what has emerged is a fragmented regulatory landscape shaped by different legal traditions, political priorities, and societal values.

To understand AI regulation today, one must move beyond statutes and examine regulatory philosophies. Broadly, three dominant approaches have emerged: the United States' adaptive and sector-based model, the European Union's structured and risk-based framework, and China's centralized and state-driven system. Each represents not just a legal strategy, but a distinct vision of how technology should interact with society.

THE STRUCTURAL PROBLEM: LAW IS LOCAL, AI IS GLOBAL

At its core, AI regulation faces a structural mismatch. Legal systems are designed to operate within defined jurisdictions, while AI systems operate across them. This creates layered challenges involving responsibility, compliance, and enforcement.

A single AI system may be trained in one country, deployed in another, and used globally. Each stage may trigger different legal obligations. The result is not a unified regulatory environment, but a convergence of overlapping expectations.[1]

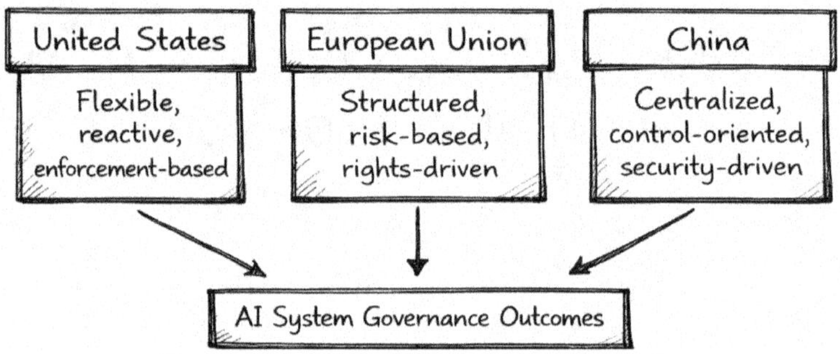

Figure 12.1: Diverging Regulatory Philosophies

THE UNITED STATES: ADAPTIVE AND SECTOR-DRIVEN REGULATION

The United States has not enacted a comprehensive AI law. Instead, it regulates AI through a network of existing legal frameworks and institutions. This reflects a long-standing feature of American governance. Technologies are not regulated in isolation but through the contexts in which they are used. The central question is not what AI is, but how it is being applied.

When AI is used in hiring, it falls under employment law. When it is used in lending, it is governed by financial regulation. When it appears in healthcare, it is subject to medical oversight. The same system may be evaluated differently depending on its function.

Regulatory agencies play a central role in this model. Consumer protection authorities address deceptive AI claims. Employment regulators examine bias in algorithmic hiring.

1. Anu Bradford, *Digital Empires: The Global Battle to Regulate Technology* (2023).

Financial regulators focus on fairness in lending. Medical authorities assess safety in clinical applications. In each case, AI is brought within the scope of existing law.

This approach provides flexibility. Regulators can respond quickly without waiting for new legislation. It allows the legal system to evolve alongside technological change. However, it also creates fragmentation. Different sectors apply different standards, and protections may vary depending on context.

Federal initiatives such as the Blueprint for an AI Bill of Rights and executive guidance attempt to provide direction. These frameworks emphasize safety, fairness, privacy, and transparency. However, they are not binding laws. Their role is to influence behavior rather than enforce compliance. The result is a system that is adaptable but uncertain. It encourages innovation while leaving gaps that may only become visible after harm occurs.

This approach is increasingly visible in ongoing litigation involving artificial intelligence. In cases such as Andersen v. Stability AI[2] and Authors Guild v. OpenAI[3], courts are being asked to apply traditional copyright principles to AI training practices. These cases illustrate how existing legal frameworks are being extended to address novel technological questions, rather than replaced entirely.

THE EUROPEAN UNION: A STRUCTURED, RISK-BASED FRAMEWORK

The European Union has taken a more deliberate approach by creating a comprehensive legal framework specifically for AI. At the center of this effort is the AI Act, which organizes regulation around the concept of risk.[4]

The EU approach begins with a recognition that not all AI systems present the same level of concern. Some systems have minimal impact, while others can affect fundamental rights and societal structures. Regulation is therefore calibrated according to risk level.

---

2. *Andersen v. Stability AI Ltd.*, No. 3:23-cv-00201 (N.D. Cal. 2023).

3. *Authors Guild v. OpenAI Inc.*, No. 1:23-cv-08292 (S.D.N.Y.) [1]

4. Regulation (EU) 2024/1689 (Artificial Intelligence Act).

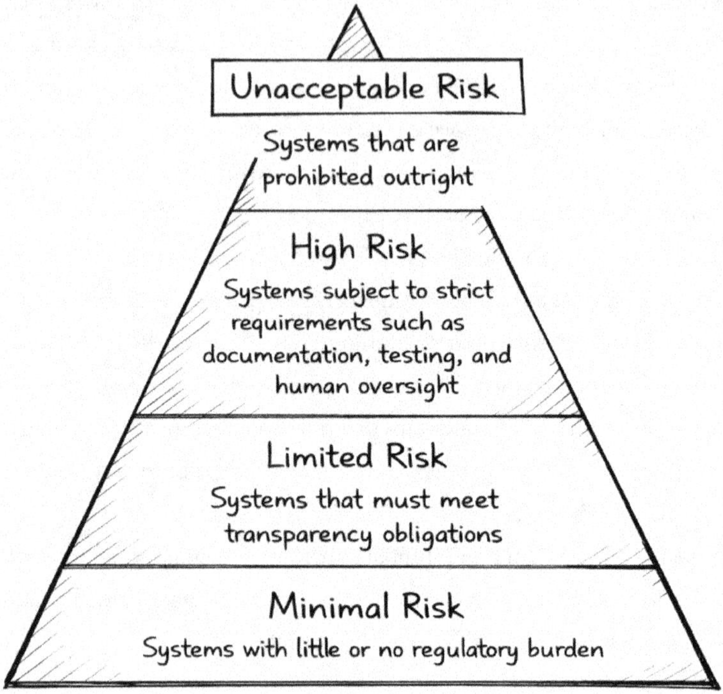

Figure 12.2: The EU Risk Pyramid

This model reflects a broader commitment within European law to the protection of fundamental rights. Privacy, fairness, and human dignity are central considerations, not secondary concerns. A defining feature of the EU approach is its reach beyond its borders. Companies that offer AI systems within the European market must comply with these rules, regardless of where they are based. This gives the framework global influence.

The EU model offers clarity and predictability. Organizations know what is expected of them based on the classification of their systems. At the same time, compliance can be demanding. Documentation, testing, and oversight requirements may slow development and increase costs.

Artificial intelligence systems are fundamentally dependent on data. As has been observed, data functions as the lifeblood of AI systems, shaping how they learn, operate, and produce outputs. This dependence on data is central to understanding why different jurisdictions regulate AI differently, particularly in areas such as privacy, intellectual property, and cross-border data flows.

The emphasis on transparency, fairness, and accountability reflects a broader regulatory philosophy that seeks to ensure that AI systems remain explainable and subject to human oversight. These principles are not merely technical requirements. They represent foundational legal values that shape how AI is governed within the European framework.

CHINA: CENTRALIZED CONTROL AND STATE-DRIVEN GOVERNANCE

China represents a third regulatory model, one that places strong emphasis on state oversight, security, and social stability.[5] In this system, AI is treated not only as an economic tool but also as an instrument with political and societal implications.

Regulation focuses on ensuring that AI systems operate within defined boundaries set by the state. Companies must register their systems, undergo security reviews, and ensure that outputs comply with established standards. Particular attention is given to generative systems and synthetic media, which must include mechanisms such as traceability and watermarking.[6]

Data governance is central to this model. Certain categories of data must remain within national borders, limiting international transfer and reinforcing state control over digital infrastructure.[7]

This approach allows for rapid implementation and strong enforcement. It aligns technological development with national priorities. At the same time, it raises questions about transparency, accountability, and the balance between control and innovation.

A WORLD OF REGULATORY COLLISION

These three approaches intersect in practice. A single AI system may be subject to multiple regulatory expectations at once. A system that complies with U.S. standards may not

---

5. China's Interim Measures for the Management of Generative Artificial Intelligence Services (2023).

6. China's Provisions on the Administration of Deep Synthesis Internet Information Services (2022).

7. Personal Information Protection Law of the People's Republic of China (PIPL) (2021).

meet European requirements. A model acceptable in Europe may need modification to operate in China. Companies operating across borders must navigate these differences carefully.

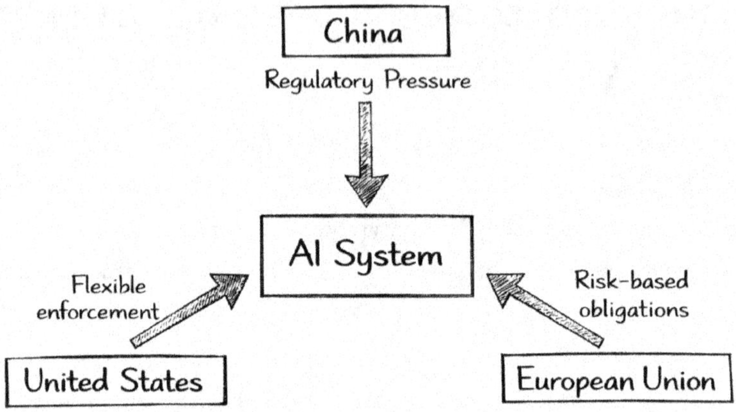

Figure 12.3: The Fragmented Regulatory Landscape

CONFLICT OF LAWS IN AI GOVERNANCE

One of the most complex challenges emerging from the global nature of artificial intelligence is the issue of conflict of laws. As AI systems operate across jurisdictions, fundamental questions arise about which legal system should govern their development, deployment, and outcomes.

An AI system may be trained in one jurisdiction, deployed in another, and produce effects in a third. Each of these stages may trigger different legal obligations, leading to overlapping or even conflicting regulatory requirements.

This creates a situation in which compliance is not merely a matter of following a single legal framework. Instead, it requires navigating multiple legal systems simultaneously, each grounded in different priorities and values.

THE EMERGING PRINCIPLE: REGULATION BY PHILOSOPHY, NOT BY TECHNOLOGY

What becomes clear across these systems is that artificial intelligence is not being regulated in a uniform way. Instead, it is being shaped by deeper legal and societal philosophies.

The same AI system can be treated as:

- A market innovation in one jurisdiction,
- A rights-sensitive tool in another, and
- A matter of state control in a third.

This reveals a critical insight. AI regulation is no longer about the technology itself. It is about the values that societies choose to embed into that technology. For practitioners, this means that compliance is not simply technical or legal. It is interpretive. One must understand not only the rules, but the reasoning behind them.

TOWARD COORDINATION OR CONTINUED FRAGMENTATION

Efforts to create shared standards are underway. International organizations have proposed principles focused on fairness, transparency, and accountability.[8] Governments are engaging in dialogue to align certain aspects of regulation. However, full harmonization remains unlikely. Regulation reflects values, and those values differ across regions. The European Union emphasizes rights and protections. The United States prioritizes flexibility and innovation. China focuses on stability and control.

These differences are not temporary. They are rooted in broader legal and political systems.

REGULATION AS A REFLECTION OF VALUES

AI regulation is not simply about rules. It is about the principles that guide how technology is developed and used. The United States shows how existing legal systems can adapt, but also highlights the challenges of fragmentation. The European Union demonstrates the power of structured regulation, while raising questions about complexity and compli-

8. OECD, OECD Principles on Artificial Intelligence (2024 update); UNESCO, Recommendation on the Ethics of Artificial Intelligence (2021).

ance. China illustrates the effectiveness of centralized oversight, alongside concerns about control and freedom.

The future of AI governance will not be defined by a single global framework. Instead, it will be shaped by the interaction of multiple systems, each reflecting its own priorities. For anyone working in this field, the key question is no longer what the law is. It is which legal system applies, and what values it represents. Understanding these differences is essential, not only for compliance, but for shaping the future of AI itself.

The regulatory approaches discussed in this chapter also interact with broader questions of liability. As AI systems become embedded in critical decision-making processes, issues such as duty of care, foreseeability, and responsibility will increasingly shape how legal systems respond to harm.

13

BUILDING A GOVERNANCE FRAMEWORK

How to Design AI Systems That Are Accountable and Trusted

Artificial Intelligence is no longer an emerging technology confined to research labs or experimental environments. It is embedded in the infrastructure of modern decision-making. It shapes hiring processes, influences access to credit, supports medical recommendations, and determines how information is distributed across digital platforms. These systems do not merely assist human decisions; in many contexts, they actively structure them.

This shift carries profound implications. When decision-making becomes partially or fully automated, the consequences are no longer limited to efficiency gains or technical performance. They extend into questions of fairness, accountability, and rights. An inaccurate recommendation system may inconvenience a user. A flawed hiring algorithm, however, can systematically exclude qualified candidates. A biased lending model can reinforce economic inequality. A poorly governed AI system does not fail in isolation; it can scale harm across entire populations.

In this context, governance becomes indispensable. It is not an external layer added after deployment, nor is it a purely legal requirement. Governance is the framework that determines how artificial intelligence systems are designed, implemented, monitored, and corrected over time. It defines who is responsible, how risks are managed, and how systems are aligned with societal expectations.

Without governance, AI systems operate in a vacuum of responsibility. Decisions become difficult to trace, accountability becomes diffused, and trust becomes fragile. Over time, this erosion of trust does not only affect individual systems; it undermines confidence in the broader technological ecosystem. Governance, therefore, is not a constraint on innovation. It is the condition that allows innovation to be sustained.

UNDERSTANDING GOVERNANCE BEYOND COMPLIANCE

A common misconception is that governance is equivalent to compliance. In reality, compliance represents only one dimension of governance. Compliance focuses on adherence to existing laws and regulations. Governance, by contrast, encompasses the broader set of structures and processes that guide how systems operate in practice.

An organization may comply with legal requirements while still deploying systems that produce harmful or unintended outcomes. Laws often lag behind technological development, and not all risks are captured within existing legal frameworks. Governance fills this gap by embedding oversight directly into the lifecycle of AI systems.

This broader understanding of governance includes internal policies, technical controls, monitoring mechanisms, documentation practices, and escalation procedures. It also includes organizational culture and decision-making processes. Governance is not only about what is required by law; it is about how responsibility is operationalized within institutions.

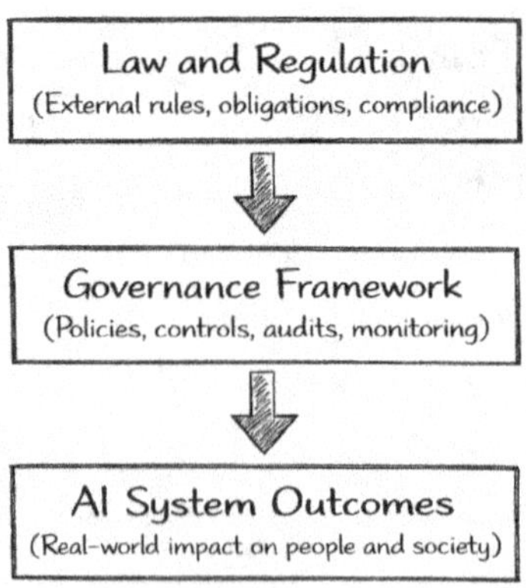

Figure 13.1: From Regulation to Governance

Core Principles:
Compliance ensures legality. Governance ensures responsibility.

Governance operates continuously. It does not begin and end with deployment. It evolves alongside the system, adapting to new data, new contexts, and new risks. This continuous nature makes governance particularly important in AI, where change is constant and uncertainty is inherent.

PRINCIPLES FOR TRUSTWORTHY AI

Across jurisdictions and institutions, a set of foundational principles has emerged as the basis for responsible AI governance.[1] These principles are not arbitrary. They reflect recurring concerns about how AI systems affect individuals and society.

Fairness requires that systems do not produce unjustified discrimination. This extends beyond outputs to include the data used for training and the assumptions embedded within models. Historical data often reflects existing inequalities. Without intervention, AI systems can reproduce and amplify those patterns.

Accountability ensures that responsibility remains identifiable. In complex systems, decisions may result from interactions between multiple components. Governance must ensure that this complexity does not obscure responsibility. There must always be a clear path to determine who is responsible for outcomes.

Transparency addresses the need for visibility. While not all systems can be fully explained in technical or non-technical terms, stakeholders must have meaningful insight into how decisions are made. Transparency supports trust, enables oversight, and allows affected individuals to challenge outcomes where necessary.

Safety and reliability focus on ensuring that systems perform as intended. This includes robustness under different conditions, resistance to manipulation, and consistency in outputs. A system that performs well in controlled environments but fails in real-world conditions cannot be considered reliable.

1. OECD, OECD Principles on Artificial Intelligence (2024 update); UNESCO, Recommendation on the Ethics of Artificial Intelligence (2021).

Human oversight ensures that automation does not eliminate responsibility. In high-stakes contexts, human judgment must remain part of the decision-making process. Oversight is not about rejecting automation; it is about ensuring that automation operates within accountable boundaries.

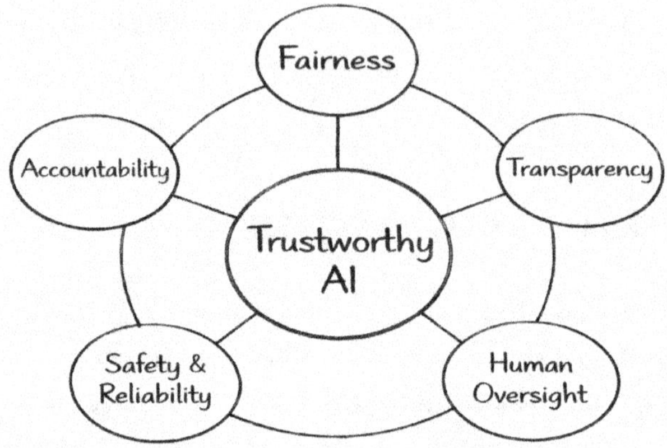

Figure 13.2: Core Principles of AI Governance

> **Critical Observation:**
> Trustworthy AI is not a feature. It is the result of multiple principles working together.

The importance of human oversight has also emerged in litigation involving the use of AI systems within legal practice itself. In *United States v. Heppner*, the court considered whether communications involving an AI system could qualify for attorney-client privilege or protection under the work-product doctrine.[2] The court emphasized that AI systems do not possess the characteristics necessary to establish confidential legal relationships in the same manner as human attorneys. This distinction reinforced the continuing importance of human judgment, professional responsibility, and confidentiality within legal processes. The case illustrates a broader governance principle: AI systems may assist professional decision-making, but they do not automatically inherit the legal protections, duties, or institutional trust associated with human professionals.

2. *United States v. Bradley Heppner* (S.D.N.Y. Feb. 17, 2026).

These principles are increasingly reflected in governance frameworks around the world. Their importance lies not in their recognition, but in their implementation. A principle that is acknowledged but not operationalized does not function as a safeguard.

TECHNICAL AND LEGAL SAFEGUARDS AS INTEGRATED SYSTEMS

Governance requires the integration of both technical and legal mechanisms. Each addresses different aspects of risk, and each compensates for the limitations of the other.

Technical safeguards operate within AI systems. They include bias testing, algorithmic auditing, explainability tools, and data security measures. These tools are designed to identify and mitigate risks during development and operation. They provide insight into how systems behave and enable corrective action when necessary.

Legal safeguards operate externally. They define acceptable conduct and establish consequences for violations. Anti-discrimination laws, privacy protections, and liability frameworks all shape how AI systems are developed and deployed. They provide the authority needed to enforce standards and address harm.

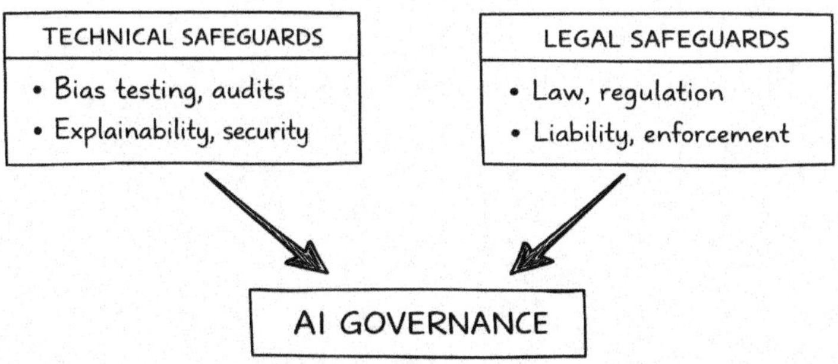

Figure 13.3: Technical and Legal Safeguards

> **Core Principles:**
> Technical safeguards manage risk. Legal safeguards enforce responsibility. Governance requires both.

The relationship between these safeguards is interdependent. Technical measures without legal backing may lack consistency and authority. Legal rules without technical implementation may remain ineffective. Governance emerges where these systems intersect.

GOVERNANCE ACROSS THE AI LIFECYCLE

Governance must be embedded throughout the entire lifecycle of an AI system. It is not a single checkpoint, but a continuous process that evolves alongside the system.

During the design phase, governance involves decisions about data selection, model architecture, and risk identification. Many risks originate at this stage. Choices about what data to include, how to structure models, and what objectives to optimize can shape outcomes in ways that are difficult to reverse.

During development, governance focuses on testing and validation. Systems must be evaluated for performance, fairness, robustness, and potential unintended effects. Documentation becomes critical at this stage, ensuring that decisions can be reviewed and understood.

During deployment, governance addresses how systems are introduced into real-world environments. This includes user training, monitoring systems, and safeguards against misuse. Deployment is where theoretical risks become practical realities.

After deployment, governance becomes a matter of continuous oversight. Systems must be monitored, audited, and updated as conditions change. New risks may emerge, requiring ongoing intervention.

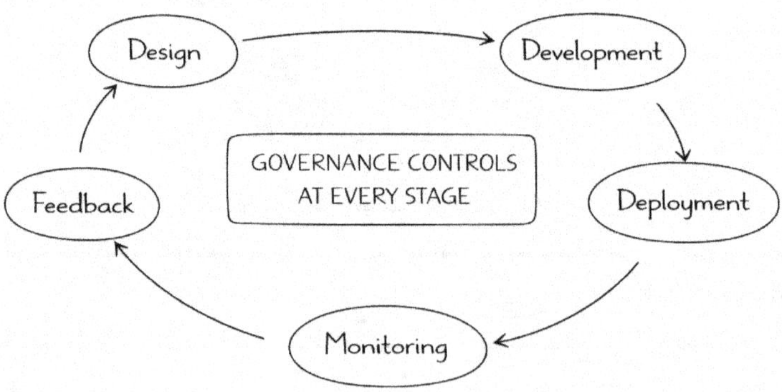

Figure 13.4: AI Governance Lifecycle

Critical Observation:

Governance is not a stage. It is a continuous cycle.

GOVERNANCE AS A SHARED RESPONSIBILITY

AI governance cannot be assigned to a single group. It requires coordination across multiple stakeholders, each contributing a different form of expertise and oversight.

Legal professionals and policymakers define the frameworks within which AI operates. They establish standards, interpret obligations, and ensure enforcement. Their role is to translate societal values into legal structures.

Technologists are responsible for embedding governance into system design. Their decisions determine how systems function at a technical level. Governance that is not built into design is often difficult to implement later.

Organizations and business leaders determine how AI is deployed in practice. Their priorities shape whether governance is treated as essential or secondary. Investment in governance reflects institutional commitment.

Civil society and the public provide oversight. They raise concerns, demand accountability, and influence the expectations that guide AI use. Their role ensures that governance remains responsive to societal needs.

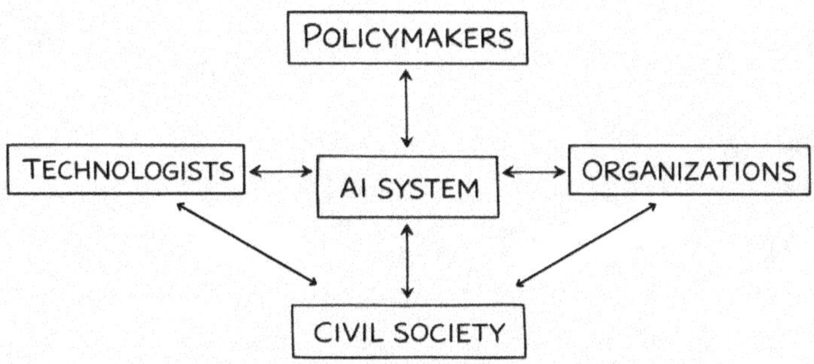

Figure 13.5: The Governance Ecosystem

Key Idea:

AI governance fails when responsibility is unclear. It succeeds when responsibility is shared and coordinated.

PROACTIVE GOVERNANCE IN A RAPIDLY EVOLVING LANDSCAPE

The pace of AI development creates a persistent gap between innovation and regulation. Systems evolve faster than legal frameworks can adapt. This makes reactive governance insufficient.

Reactive governance responds after harm occurs. It relies on enforcement and correction. While necessary, it is often too late to prevent damage. A more effective approach is proactive governance, which anticipates risks and embeds safeguards before deployment.

Critical Observation:
Reactive governance responds to harm. Proactive governance prevents it.

Proactive governance requires foresight. It involves identifying potential risks early, designing systems with safeguards, and continuously monitoring outcomes. It shifts the focus from correction to prevention.

GOVERNANCE AS THE FOUNDATION OF TRUST

Artificial intelligence will continue to evolve. Its capabilities will expand, and its applications will become more integrated into everyday life. The question is not whether this evolution will occur, but how it will be guided.

Governance provides the structure through which AI systems can operate responsibly. It ensures that principles are translated into practice, that risks are managed, and that responsibility is clearly defined. Without governance, the potential benefits of AI are undermined by uncertainty and risk.

The future of AI depends not only on what can be built, but on how it is governed. Building governance frameworks rooted in fairness, accountability, transparency, and oversight ensures that artificial intelligence serves society in a way that is sustainable, responsible, and worthy of trust.

14

BRIDGING THE DIVIDE

What It Takes to Align Law, Technology, and Society

Artificial intelligence is not waiting for the law to catch up. It is already embedded in systems that shape human lives in ways that are immediate, consequential, and often invisible. Each day, algorithmic systems influence who is hired, who gains access to financial resources, what medical advice is followed, and how individuals are evaluated across digital environments. These systems do not merely assist decision-making. They structure it, often at a scale and speed that exceeds human oversight.

The implications of this shift extend far beyond efficiency. When decision-making becomes partially or fully automated, the consequences move into the domain of rights, fairness, and accountability. A flawed recommendation system may inconvenience a user, but a flawed hiring system can systematically exclude entire groups. A biased credit model can reinforce structural inequality across thousands of decisions. In such contexts, risk is not episodic. It becomes systemic.

This is the defining governance challenge of the present moment. The pace of technological advancement has outstripped the capacity of traditional governance structures to respond. Legal systems, by design, evolve incrementally through interpretation, precedent, and institutional deliberation. Artificial intelligence evolves continuously through iteration, deployment, and data feedback loops. This mismatch creates a persistent gap, and within that gap, risk accumulates.

The Governance Gap:
When technology moves faster than law, risk does not pause. It scales.

THE NECESSITY OF BRIDGING AI AND LAW

Artificial intelligence and law cannot function as separate domains. They are not parallel systems that occasionally intersect. They are interdependent structures that must evolve together if either is to remain effective.

Legal systems provide structure, accountability, and protection. They define the boundaries within which technological systems operate and establish mechanisms for redress when harm occurs. Without legal frameworks, technological systems lack constraint and direction. At the same time, technological systems define the environments in which legal principles are applied. They shape the contexts in which rights are exercised, obligations arise, and decisions are made. Without an understanding of these systems, legal rules risk becoming disconnected from the realities they are meant to govern. This interdependence creates a shared responsibility.

For legal professionals, this means moving beyond passive interpretation of technological outcomes. It requires engaging with how systems are designed, how decisions are generated, and where risks emerge within the system lifecycle. Legal expertise must expand to include technological awareness, not as a specialization, but as a practical necessity.

For technologists, responsibility begins at the point of design. Systems are not neutral. They reflect the assumptions embedded in datasets, the objectives defined during development, and the trade-offs made during optimization. Designing responsibly requires anticipating how systems will behave in real-world contexts and how those behaviors may affect different groups. Governance cannot be imposed after deployment. It must be built into the system itself.

Organizations and institutions translate these responsibilities into practice. Their decisions determine whether governance is treated as essential or secondary. Investment in compliance, risk management, and ethical system design reflects institutional priorities. When governance is embedded into strategy, it becomes a driver of trust rather than a constraint on innovation.

Civil society and the public complete this structure. Their role is not passive. Through advocacy, participation, and oversight, they shape the expectations that guide how AI systems are deployed and evaluated. Governance is not solely institutional. It is societal.

The Central Truth:

Law without technology becomes outdated. Technology without law becomes dangerous. The future requires both.

FROM AWARENESS TO RESPONSIBILITY

Recognizing the need for governance is only the first step. The more significant challenge lies in translating awareness into responsibility. This requires a shift in how each actor within the AI ecosystem understands their role.

For lawyers, this means expanding beyond outcome-based analysis. Legal evaluation must extend into processes, architectures, and data flows.[1] It requires the ability to question not only what a system produces, but how it produces it. This shift transforms legal practice from reactive assessment to proactive engagement.

For technologists, responsibility is inseparable from design. Every dataset selected, every model trained, and every system deployed contributes to downstream outcomes. These decisions shape who benefits, who is excluded, and how risks are distributed. Responsible design requires anticipating these effects and incorporating safeguards before systems are deployed at scale.

For organizations, responsibility lies in implementation. Policies, governance frameworks, and oversight mechanisms determine whether principles translate into practice. Without institutional commitment, governance remains aspirational rather than operational.

For society, responsibility lies in engagement. Public expectations, regulatory pressure, and social norms influence how systems are built and used. Governance is strengthened when these forces operate together.

Responsibility, in this context, is not abstract. It is distributed across the system.

---

1. Andrew D. Selbst et al., *Deconstructing Design Decisions: Why Courts Must Interrogate Machine Learning and Other Technologies* (2024). [11, 13]

THE FUTURE REQUIRES DELIBERATE DESIGN

The trajectory of artificial intelligence will not be determined solely by technological capability. It will be shaped by the choices made about how that capability is governed. These choices must be deliberate, coordinated, and grounded in clear principles.

Reactive governance is insufficient for systems that operate at scale.[2] Waiting for harm to occur before responding allows risk to propagate across populations. Proactive governance, by contrast, anticipates risk and integrates safeguards into system design before deployment. This approach requires foresight and a willingness to act in conditions of uncertainty.

Global coordination introduces an additional layer of complexity.[3] Artificial intelligence systems operate across borders, while legal systems remain largely national. This creates inconsistencies that can undermine both enforcement and trust. While full harmonization may not be feasible, alignment across core principles is necessary to ensure coherence.

At the center of these efforts must be a commitment to foundational values. Fairness, accountability, transparency, and human dignity cannot remain abstract ideals.[4] They must be operationalized within systems, embedded into design processes, and reflected in governance frameworks.

> **The Future Is Shaped by Design and Choice:**
> AI will shape the world. The question is whether we shape AI first.

---

2. NIST, *AI Risk Management Framework* (2023).

3. UNESCO Recommendation on the Ethics of Artificial Intelligence (2021).

4. OECD, OECD Principles on Artificial Intelligence (2024 update); European Commission, *Ethics Guidelines for Trustworthy AI* (2019).

FROM FRAGMENTATION TO ALIGNMENT

One of the most significant risks in AI governance is fragmentation. When systems, institutions, and jurisdictions operate without coordination, gaps emerge. These gaps create uncertainty, reduce accountability, and increase the likelihood of harm.

Alignment does not require uniformity. Different jurisdictions may adopt different regulatory approaches based on their legal traditions and societal priorities. However, alignment requires a shared understanding of core principles and a commitment to ensuring that systems operate within acceptable boundaries.

This alignment must occur across multiple levels. Legal frameworks must connect with technical standards.[5] Organizational practices must align with regulatory expectations. Societal values must inform system design. Governance is not a single structure. It is a network of interconnected elements that must function together.

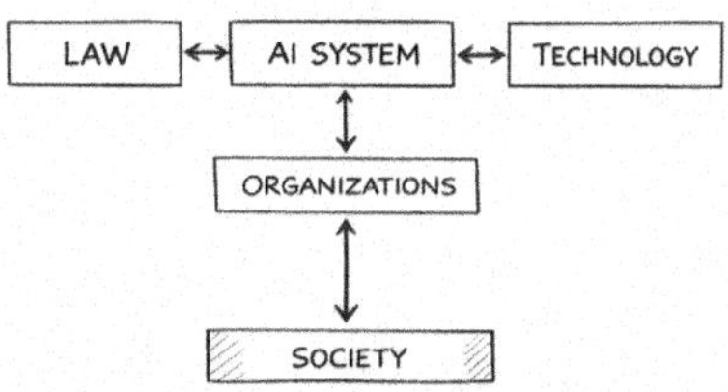

Figure 14.1: Bridging AI and Law

The future of artificial intelligence is not predetermined. It will not be defined solely by advances in computational power or model sophistication. It will be shaped by the frameworks that guide how these systems are developed, deployed, and governed.

The question is not whether artificial intelligence will continue to evolve. It will. The question is whether that evolution will be guided with intention or allowed to unfold without sufficient oversight. Bridging artificial intelligence and law is not only a professional responsibility. It is a societal imperative. It requires collaboration across disciplines, coordination across institutions, and a commitment to values that extend beyond efficiency and innovation.

5. Regulation (EU) 2024/1689 (Artificial Intelligence Act).

The systems being built today will define the structures of tomorrow. The decisions made now will determine whether artificial intelligence reinforces trust or undermines it, whether it expands opportunity or deepens inequality.

Principle:

The future of artificial intelligence will not be decided by machines. It will be decided by the frameworks we build and the responsibility we choose to exercise.

15

SPEAKING THE SAME LANGUAGE

Translating Between Law and Artificial Intelligence

Artificial intelligence and law do not only operate with different tools. They operate with different languages. These differences are not superficial. They shape how problems are understood, how risks are identified, and how decisions are made.

A technologist describing a system may refer to models, training data, inference, and optimization. A lawyer examining the same system may speak of liability, evidence, compliance, and due process. Both may be analyzing the same phenomenon, yet they are often speaking past each other.

This disconnect is not simply a communication problem. It is a structural barrier. When language does not align, understanding breaks down. When understanding breaks down, risk increases. Bridging artificial intelligence and law therefore requires more than technical knowledge or legal expertise. It requires translation.

> **Key Insight:**
> Misalignment in language produces misalignment in judgment.

WHY LANGUAGE MATTERS IN AI GOVERNANCE

Language determines how systems are framed. When a technologist describes a model as "accurate," the reference point is often statistical performance. When a lawyer hears the same word, the concern may shift to reliability, admissibility, or defensibility. The same term carries different meanings depending on the discipline.

This divergence becomes critical in high-stakes environments. A system that is technically efficient may still be legally problematic. A process that appears compliant may still be technically flawed. Without a shared understanding of terms, these gaps remain hidden.

Language also shapes responsibility. The way a system is described influences how accountability is assigned. If a decision is framed as "automated," responsibility may appear diffuse. If it is framed as "designed," responsibility becomes more clearly attributable. Clarity in language is therefore not cosmetic. It is foundational.

FROM TERMINOLOGY TO TRANSLATION

The goal of this chapter is not to provide exhaustive definitions. It is to create a working translation between two domains.

Each concept below is presented in three layers:

- **AI Term:** How it is used in technical contexts
- **Legal Interpretation:** How it translates into legal relevance
- **Practical Meaning:** What it actually implies in real-world use

PART I: CORE AI TERMS FOR LEGAL PROFESSIONALS

MODEL:

AI Context: A system trained on data to identify patterns and generate outputs.

Legal Interpretation: A decision-making mechanism whose behavior must be explainable, reviewable, and potentially attributable.

Practical Meaning: This is the "engine" producing outcomes. If it fails, the question becomes: who is responsible?

TRAINING DATA:

AI Context: The dataset used to train a model.

Legal Interpretation: A potential source of bias, infringement, or unlawful use.

Practical Meaning: If the data is flawed or unlawfully obtained, the entire system is compromised.

BIAS:

AI Context: Systematic error in predictions.

Legal Interpretation: Potential discrimination or unequal treatment under the law.

Practical Meaning: Bias is not just a technical issue. It can become a legal violation.

INFERENCE:

AI Context: The process of generating outputs from a trained model.

Legal Interpretation: The moment a system produces a decision that may carry legal consequences.

Practical Meaning: This is where risk becomes real.

BLACK BOX MODEL:

AI Context: A model whose internal reasoning is not easily interpretable.

Legal Interpretation: A system that may fail standards of explainability or admissibility.

Practical Meaning: If you cannot explain it, you may not be able to defend it.

PART II: LEGAL TERMS FOR AI PROFESSIONALS

LIABILITY:

Legal Context: Legal responsibility for harm or wrongdoing.

AI Translation: Responsibility assigned across the system lifecycle (design, deployment, use).

Practical Meaning: If your system causes harm, the question is not whether it worked, but who answers for it.

DUE PROCESS:

Legal Context: Fair procedures before decisions affecting rights are made.

AI Translation: Systems must allow for challenge, review, and explanation.

Practical Meaning: People must be able to question AI decisions that affect them.

ADMISSIBLITY:

Legal Context: Whether evidence can be accepted in court.

AI Translation: Whether outputs from AI systems can be trusted and verified.

Practical Meaning: Not all AI outputs are usable as evidence.

STANDARD OF PROOF:

Legal Context: The level of certainty required to establish a claim.

AI Translation: The reliability threshold required for AI-generated outputs.

Practical Meaning: High-stakes decisions require higher confidence.

NEGLIGENCE:

Legal Context: Failure to exercise reasonable care.

AI Translation: Failure to design, test, or deploy systems responsibly.

Practical Meaning: Poor system design can become legal fault.

PART III: SHARED CONCEPTS (WHERE LAW AND AI MEET)

EXPLAINABILITY:

AI: Ability to interpret model outputs

Law: Ability to justify decisions

Reality: Without explanation, trust collapses

ACCOUNTABILITY:

AI: System traceability

Law: Assigning responsibility

Reality: Someone must answer

FAIRNESS:

AI: Statistical parity

Law: Equal treatment

Reality: Outcomes must not disadvantage protected groups

TRANSPARENCY:

AI: Visibility into system design

Law: Disclosure obligations

Reality: Hidden systems create risk

BUILDING A WORKING LANGUAGE

The purpose of this chapter is not mastery. It is fluency. Lawyers do not need to become engineers. Engineers do not need to become lawyers. But both must become conversant enough to engage meaningfully with the systems they build, regulate, or challenge.

A shared language reduces friction. It enables more effective collaboration, clearer analysis, and more precise accountability. It allows each discipline to ask better questions and recognize risks earlier. Without this shared language, the gap persists. With it, alignment becomes possible.

Closing Insight:

Bridging law and artificial intelligence is not only about systems. It is about understanding. And understanding begins with language.

About the Author

Tolulope Awoyomiis a lawyer, researcher, and artificial intelligence educator passionate about helping people understand the rapidly changing world of technology. She holds an LL.B. in Law from Babcock University, an LL.M. in Business and Finance Law from The George Washington University School of Law, a Master of Science in Information Systems Technology, a Graduate Certificate in Artificial Intelligence from The George Washington University, and a Professional Certificate in Artificial Intelligence and Machine Learning from the Massachusetts Institute of Technology (MIT). Her academic journey reflects her deep interest in how technology and law shape the world around us.

Tolulope has spent more than seven years working across legal research, technology education, AI governance, and innovation leadership. Over the years, she has taught students, professionals, and organizations how to understand and use artificial intelligence with confidence. She speaks and teaches on topics such as responsible AI, information systems, data literacy, and the future of work. Whether she is teaching in a classroom, leading a workshop, or guiding community learners, her goal is always the same: to make complex ideas easier to understand.

She is the founder of AI & Law Bridge and AI for Everyone Africa, two initiatives focused on expanding access to AI education and helping people and communities adapt to emerging technologies. With her background in both law and technology, she brings a unique perspective that allows her to explain complex topics clearly and practically.

Tolulope is also the host of the *Everything AI & Law Podcast*, where she interviews experts, innovators, and thought leaders shaping the future of artificial intelligence. Alongside these conversations, she teaches listeners how AI works by breaking down theories, concepts, risks, data protection principles, and practical tools. Her ability to make AI feel approachable and relevant has helped the podcast reach listeners from around the world.

She is the author of *The Simple Book of AI* and *Bridging AI and Law*, two accessible yet insightful works that demystify artificial intelligence and its growing influence on society, decision-making, and modern institutions. Her writing equips readers with a clear understanding of how AI systems function, how they shape real-world outcomes, and why the relationship between technological innovation and legal governance has become increasingly important in an AI-driven world.

Tolulope continues to create educational resources, training programs, and research projects that promote responsible innovation and help people prepare for the opportunities and challenges of the AI era.

For more about Tolulope, visit tolulopeawoyomi.com

Connect with Tolulope on LinkedIn: https://www.linkedin.com/in/tolulope-awoyomi/

Amazon Author page: amazon.com/author/tolulopeawoyomi

www.ingramcontent.com/pod-product-compliance
Lightning Source LLC
LaVergne TN
LVHW022229200926
848481LV00006B/2184
* 9 7 9 8 9 9 9 6 7 7 4 5 7 *